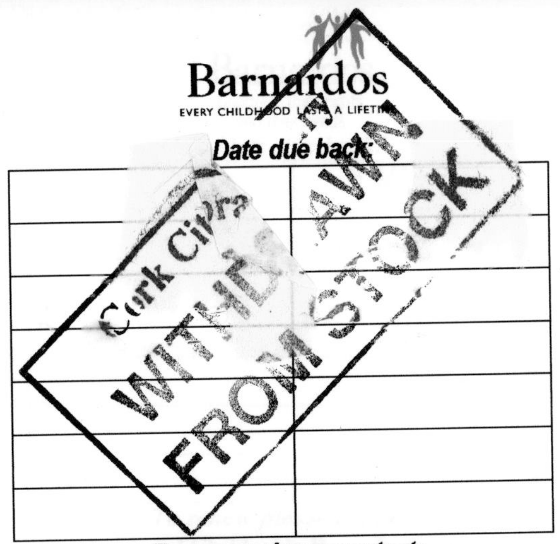

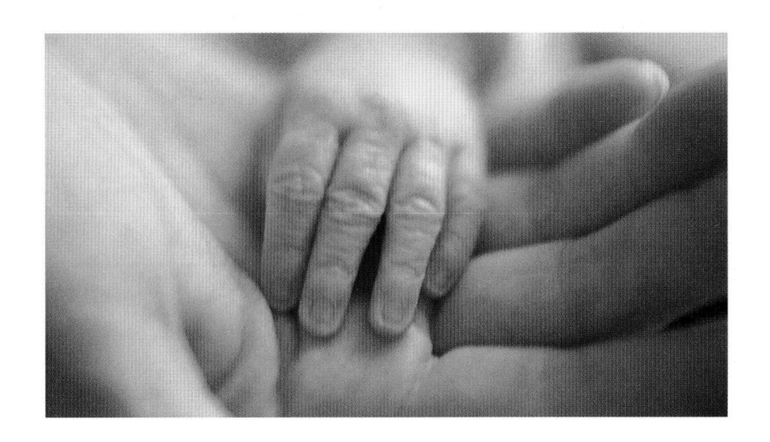

We had wanted you and waited for you,
imagined you and dreamed about you
and now that you are here,
no dream can do justice to you.

Fergal Keane, *Letter to Daniel*

love laughter *and* parenting

in the years from birth to six

Steve and Shaaron Biddulph

A Dorling Kindersley Book

LONDON, NEW YORK, SYDNEY, DELHI, PARIS,
MUNICH AND JOHANNESBURG

SENIOR MANAGING EDITOR Corinne Roberts

SENIOR MANAGING ART EDITOR Lynne Brown

SENIOR EDITOR Dawn Bates

ART EDITOR Mercedes Morgan

DESIGNERS
Glenda Fisher Dawn Young

DTP Rajen Shah

PRODUCTION
Maryann Rogers

First published in Great Britain in 2000 by
Dorling Kindersley Limited,
9 Henrietta Street, London WC2E 8PS

A CIP catalogue record for this book is available from the British Library

ISBN 0-7513-0851-X

Reproduced by Colourscan
Printed and bound in Italy by LEGO

See our complete
catalogue at
www.dk.com

AUTHORS' NOTE

The authors believe that parents, in consultation with other parents and suitable resource people, are the best equipped to decide, and are responsible for the choices they make in caring for and raising their children. The ideas and methods described in this book are suggestions and options offered from the lives and experiences of other parents. No special expertise or authority is claimed by the authors for these ideas. Readers should use their own good judgement in deciding which ideas to adopt or carry out in their own family.

Contents

A NOTE ABOUT "HE", "SHE" AND "THEM"

Once upon a time, childrearing books referred to all children as "he" (as if little girls did not matter). Then books started using "he or she", which was awkward, or alternating "he" and "she", which meant they were wrong 50 per cent of the time. We think the English language needs improving, so have written the book the way people speak – such as, "if your baby cries, you can pick them up and comfort them". In other words, "them" is used as a singular pronoun. We wanted to let you know that we are reforming the language and not just using bad grammar. We hope this makes for smooth reading.

For mothers, a welcome from Shaaron...

In a popular women's magazine there is a page in which women write about their problems and other readers suggest solutions. One letter really caught my eye as it was so easy to identify with. A young mother called Clara with three small children wrote that she had lost the ability to have fun. She felt isolated, inadequate and angry, and was starting to hate being a parent. She "knew it was supposed to be better than this" and wanted help.

The replies from mothers around the country showed that they understood well how Clara was feeling. One mother, also with three children, guessed that Clara could be caught in a vicious circle, hating herself for her angry outbursts, feeling guilty for not living up to an impossible ideal. She knew this feeling because she had "been there". She had solved the problem by changing her attitude, becoming kinder and gentler to herself. To her surprise, she found that this kindness and tolerance passed itself on to the children. She wondered whether this could, perhaps, work for Clara too.

Other women suggested making time to have more fun with the children, and relaxing her high expectations. They reminded Clara of the need to have breaks for herself. Others suggested taking vitamin B for stress, playing sport, and so on. These were practical and "road-tested" ideas, offered respectfully, with a large dose of understanding and encouragement thrown in. It was as if a caring group of down-to-earth mothers was physically gathering around Clara to bear her up and give her strength. No doctor, journalist, child development lecturer or any kind of expert could give this kind of help. These were women who had lived through what they were talking about. The conclusion is clear – to succeed in our chosen purpose, we mothers need help from other mothers (and fathers from other fathers).

That's the kind of book this is – non-expert, conveying support and suggestions from parent to parent. Everything in it has been gleaned from parents' experience, some recent and some going back generations. The aim is to make you feel surrounded by friends who respect your judgement, but can offer vast experience and helpful clues for raising your children.

For fathers, a greeting from Steve...

There's a feeling I want to tell you about. It arrives the second you know you're going to be a father, and it never quite goes away. It's made up mostly of happiness, but mixed in with a fair amount of fear. This feeling is called "being alive".

A couple of hundred years ago, families often had nine or ten children, and everyone got pretty casual about it. For a third of new parents today, the first baby they ever hold in their arms is their own baby. The unpreparedness, and the strangeness of being a father for the first time, can scare you and make you want to back away.

So right from the start you have a choice. You can back off and leave it mostly to your spouse, while you just work to pay the bills. Or you can be a hands-on, sleeves-rolled-up dad who gets in there and discovers he can do it. The more you get involved with babies and children, the more engrossing and exciting fatherhood is. There's nothing that matches it for fun, pride and terror! First-time parenthood is the emotional equivalent of bungee jumping.

There's something else – a secret every parent finds out eventually. We have kids for our own sakes. By doing our best for them, we are doing the best for ourselves. Parenthood makes you a better person (and we are talking "character development" here, not good looks). *By the time your children are raised, you may be five times the man you would have been if you'd stayed childless.* In fact, you could almost say that fatherhood makes a man of you. It makes you able to see the big picture, and able to put someone else's needs before your own. Most fathers say they would readily give up their life to save their child's. If a lion was about to eat your child, you'd jump in front. Whereas with your spouse, you'd probably toss a coin!

Anyhow (moving right along!), to sum up:

★ remember, however good a mother your partner is, your child needs you too
★ remember you are the successful descendant of ten thousand successful fathers (or you wouldn't be here at all)
★ remember you find the way by getting lost, many times
★ remember to hold hands crossing the road, and check the bottle has cooled before you stick it into your baby's mouth!

Very best wishes,

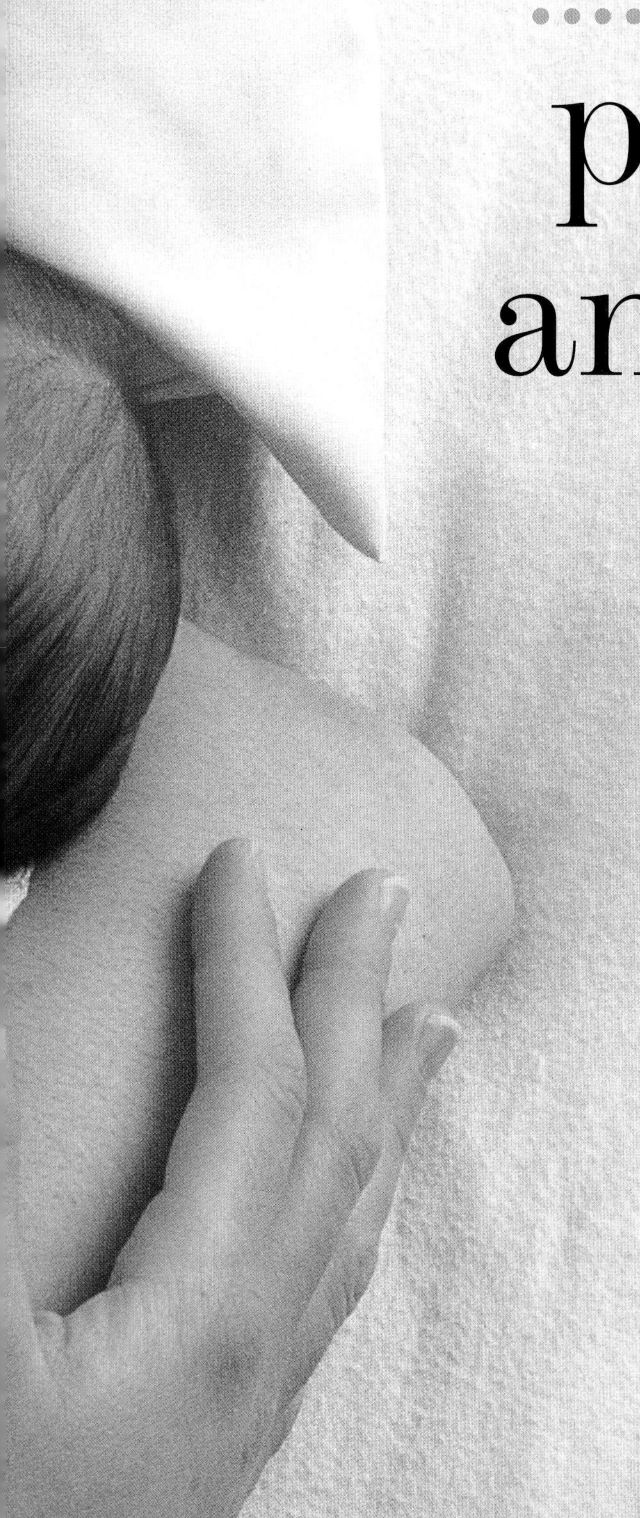

chapter 1

parenting and why it matters

The Precious Years

LOVE, LAUGHTER AND PARENTING is a book about the first six years of life. We call these "the precious years" because the foundations of trust and confidence are being laid down that will affect all the years to come. Your child will never need as much of you as during these tender and dependent times.

These years are precious for you too. No stage of life will change you as much or do so much to make you a better person. The care of little children changes you from having a teenage perspective (living mostly for yourself) to being a real adult who knows how to care for others. Your "joy levels" will soar as you experience the freshness and heart-melting trust of little children, and when these years are over you will always look back on them with longing.

Before we get all gooey though, let's be clear that this is also the hardest time – physically – in the whole family life cycle. It's a fitness marathon as you go without sleep, have little time for yourself, and have to fit your life around the uncompromising needs of a baby, toddler or pre-schooler.

In the way we live now – often distant from family and even friends – we parents need help of three kinds. We need *practical advice* and clues on what to do. We need *inspiration* that it is all worthwhile and has a purpose. We need *to feel connected* to other parents and their joys and struggles so that we can feel that we are normal and that we have friends around us.

So, in this book we have tried to include not only information, but also real-life stories, parent-lore and even the whacky humour parents use to survive.

The book includes:

★ help in communicating and teaching your child throughout the ***five stages of early childhood***:

1 Pregnancy

2 *Babe-in-arms*

3 Mobile baby

4 *Toddler*

5 Pre-school child

What to expect, what to do and how to enjoy each stage.

★ over 30 ***activity boxes*** that suggest practical games, actions or ideas suitable for a child of a particular age

★ ***true-life stories*** and examples of how parents just like you overcame or dealt with challenges or breakthroughs with their children

★ ***the world's best parenting jokes,*** because sometimes you just have to laugh

★ a special ***father's diary*** – scattered throughout the book are excerpts from the beautiful diary kept by Australian sports writer, Martin Flanagan, about his children growing up.

There's something to get clear right from the start. This book is about real children and real parents – sticky, wrinkly and fallible, as well as beautiful, loving and special. If those glossy magazine fashion spreads and "you-can-have-it-all" articles have been making you feel doubtful and inadequate, then you can relax. This book is about how it *really* is. For instance:

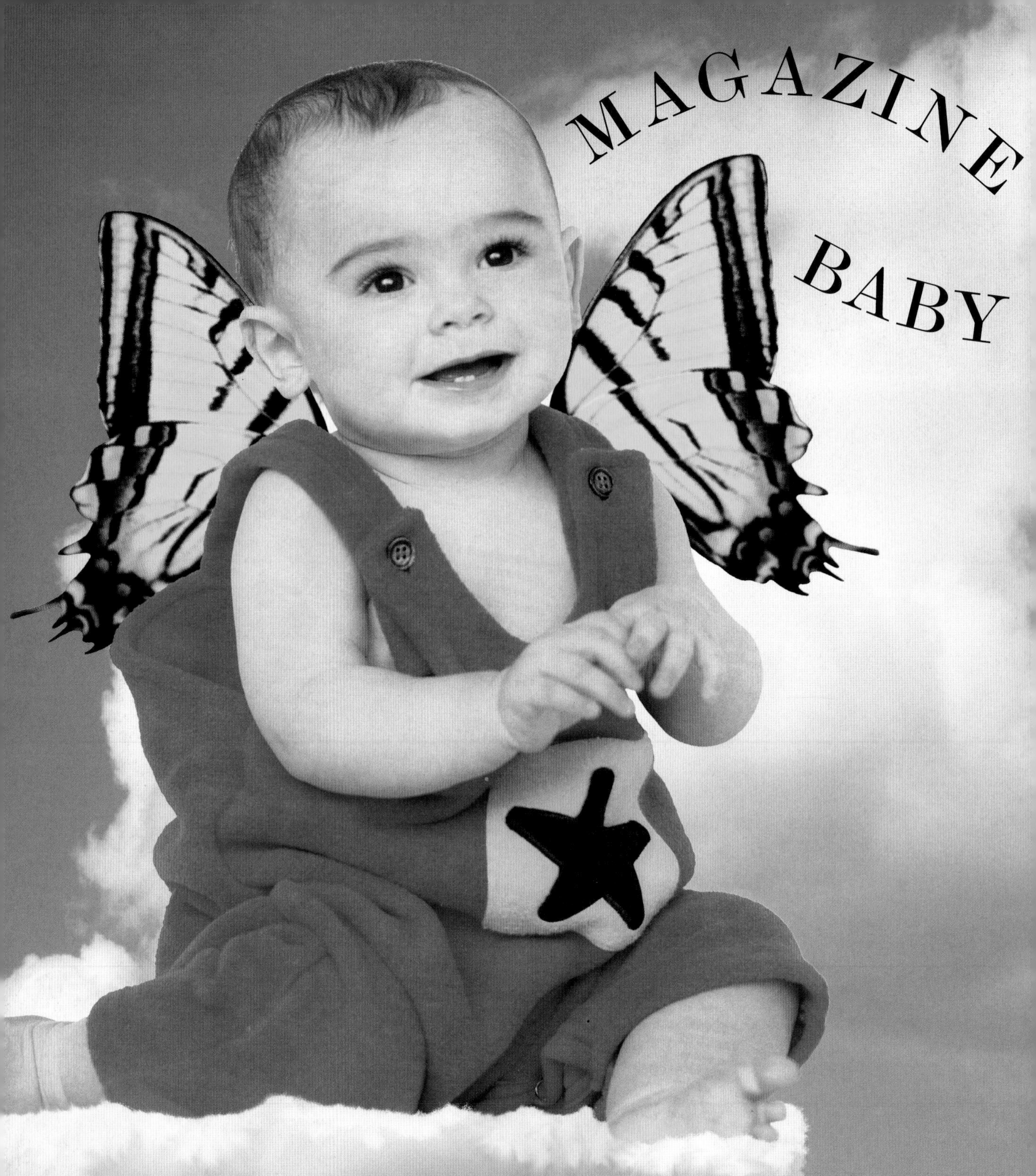

looks like an angel ....

smells of roses ....

sleeps 10 hours a night ....

proves you are a genius parent ....

wins baby contest ....

.... looks like Winston Churchill

.... *smells of you-know-what!*

.... **sleeps 10 minutes a night**

.... ***proves you are an incompetent idiot***

.... wins your heart forever!

The ideal family–ha!

Even more harmful than the myth of the perfect baby is the myth of the perfect family!

There have been several versions of this in living memory. Back in the 50's (perhaps as a reaction to the horrors of World War Two, and helped by the arrival of the family car) the idea of living in suburbia, with a picket fence, two lovely children, mum with scones and dad with briefcase, seemed like a good idea at the time. The problem – well, it was lonely for one thing. No relatives for miles, mothers going mad at home, and fathers away at work all day. The most commonly prescribed drug back then was Valium.

Then came the 80's and 90's. Women were breaking out of role expectations, but somehow society added some new ones – now you had to earn a living, be great looking, have a power career, AND have happy kids and a perfect home. Men kind of drifted, felt bad, and worked even longer hours – or were unemployed. Now the most prescribed drug was Prozac, (and Ritalin for the kids). We had swapped total boredom for total stress.

Of course some people had great lives during these decades – but they did so by resisting the pressure of the times, the advertizing, the rush to earn and spend – and by being more true to themselves.

As we enter the 21st century, we are valuing family life in its many varied shapes and sizes. Children need committed adults and those adults need friendship, strength and support from others. Instead of lonely little survival units, desperately trying to purchase happiness by working ever longer hours, we are finding new ways. You can be a single parent, or married, or gay, or disabled, or unemployed or childless, and still be a part of a network where you feel included and valued.

We are finding new ways to have community and share the joys of children, and so have more convivial lives. What we are discovering is what our ancestors knew all along: that a healthy family is a connected family.

2000+

Are we ready for a baby?

Every time you make love, there is a chance you'll get pregnant. It's quite possible for a couple to have 10–20 babies in the course of an (exhausting!) lifetime. The fact that so few people have families this big, means that lots of us exercise some choice!

Perhaps this is our first real responsibility in parenthood – to time and space our pregnancies as wisely as we can. There are times in anyone's life when to become pregnant would be a real crisis. Let's say you were really sick, were having huge fights with your partner, your mother had just died, you already had three children under five, the bank was about to throw you out of your house, and the weather forecast was for hurricanes! This might not be a good time to get pregnant! Though you do sometimes hear of someone conceiving a child at a supposedly bad time and yet everything turning out just fine.

Waiting for the right time, the right partner, some financial security, and the right place to live, might make the difference between an easier life or more of a struggle for you and your kids. Yet, if you wait for everything to be perfect, you could both be 80! It's a difficult decision. In this section we'll help you evaluate the pros and cons for yourself.

People give many reasons for their decision:

- ★ "I wanted to have my children while I was young and had lots of energy"
- ★ "I wanted to wait until I had earned some money"
- ★ "All my friends were having babies"
- ★ "I needed to see a bit more of life before I settled down"
- ★ "I wanted to find a place with a garden first, so my child could play outside".

From these few examples, you can see why this is such a personal decision. You have to really know your own mind and heart, since this is a choice for the rest of your life. Many factors come into play. Your relationship with your partner, your finances and your health all come into it. Where you are in your career, education or other life goals, your housing, and the support systems around you. Life is full of surprises, but if you have enough of these things going for you, then you can be buffered should one aspect of your life disintegrate suddenly.

“*We put all our savings into a business that crashed, and we lost everything overnight. We had a mortgage, and two young children. If it wasn't for living in a small town with lots of help from family and friends, and a place to live, we would never have coped.*”

Jill, 41 and John, 46

Talking to your partner

If you are feeling uncertain about having a baby, try the mixed feelings exercise shown below. But be sure to explain to your partner what you are doing, so that he is not totally bewildered! It helps if you indicate that your feelings are temporary, "*Today* I feel like being the parent of five kids" and "*Right now*, I'm really happy there's just the two of us."

You will rarely be absolutely 100 per cent sure. Many women who are in labour for the first time spontaneously exclaim, "Let's not have a baby! I think I'd rather wait for a year or two!" What matters is that when feelings are expressed like this, they are out and gone! If we sit on such reservations and mood swings and think, "Oh, I shouldn't think that!", then we can end up in a knot of squashed feelings.

Good things to try

The mixed-feelings exercise

Is this you? Sometimes you feel like you'd give anything to have a baby. Then the next day you are so glad to be free, able to go out to dinner or the cinema, stay out late without having to worry about childcare problems? Then you see a mother caring for her gorgeous baby or a cute, loving toddler and you seethe with jealousy. Or you see someone struggling with a screaming angry kid and you think, "Thank God that's not me." What can you do when you have these swings in your feelings? Perhaps you could try this exercise...

Whenever you are in two minds about a decision in your life, don't just toss a coin or rush into one of the two options. You must never ignore mixed feelings, as they often indicate that you are in a transition time, a time when you are gradually changing from one stage of life to another. It's important to respect this process and go very slowly.

The secret of navigating through a transition time is to take small steps and explore each aspect of the dilemma. For example, on a day when you are feeling really "clucky" and wishing you had a baby, do something small but symbolic, as if you were already pregnant. Perhaps you could:

★ ***browse in a baby shop***
★ ***think of names you like and make a list***
★ ***buy some booties***
★ ***plan a space in your bedroom where you could put a cot***
★ ***start exercising regularly***

Even if you are definite about wanting a baby, talk about it a lot with your partner, so you can express what it is you both actually envisage. Share your dreams (and fears) so that you can begin to find which ones you have in common. Talk about your hopes – the fun you will have being in the company of a little person, the challenges and the intrigue of what your child will be like, the joys of seeing them mature into a toddler, a school child, a teenager and adult.

Perhaps you and your partner may want a child for different reasons or look forward to different stages of parenting. Sometimes men are keen to have a child they can do things with, while women might yearn for a little dependent babe. These differences can be very compatible if they are out in the open and able to be talked about.

- *visit your GP and ask what you could do to prepare yourself for pregnancy*
- *volunteer to babysit for a friend*
- *find out about health insurance*
- *quit smoking and interrupt habits that could badly affect the pregnancy.*

Then, on a day when you are thinking, "No, maybe it's best I don't have a child right now" do something small but symbolic, as if you were *not going to become pregnant*:

- *plan a future career*
- *test drive the car you've always wanted*
- *collect holiday brochures*
- *talk to a friend who has chosen to be childless*
- *go on a hike by yourself*
- *dress up and have coffee and cake in a really elegant cafe*
- *have a long morning bath.*

When you continue to express each side of your ambivalence, it allows for a natural decision to occur. Over a few weeks, it will become evident that you are having many more days of wanting a baby, or many more days when you are enjoying being child-free.

All big decisions are probably best made this way, since they allow us to actively bring out our unconscious feelings, until we know in our bones what is really right for us.

If you're unsure about having a baby, volunteer to babysit for a friend.

When fears are holding you back

Talk to your partner also about the negative possibilities – what if the baby cries all the time, won't sleep, has feeding trouble, or more serious health problems? However small and niggling – or ridiculous and fanciful – these ideas are in your mind and need to be aired.

If one of you wants a child and the other doesn't, take time to go into why this is so. Sometimes one partner may be frightened to have children because they think the in-laws will try to take over when there's a baby on the scene. Both of you might want your child to be cared for at home, but be unable to see a practical way to do this because you need two incomes or just don't want to stop working. Sometimes misgivings like these are simply worked out through talking. At other times, much research and soul-searching is needed.

Some parents have fears about a baby dying, being abnormal or very sick; or the birth being difficult. Again, these concerns and their implications are best talked about. We've found that sometimes these fears mysteriously affect a couple's fertility, and once resolved the couple go ahead to conceive naturally without assistance. You can also seek more information – genetic counselling, advice about pregnancy at your age, more realistic information about disabilities and differences in children. By meeting and talking to parents with high-need children, you may realize the preciousness of life in all its variations, and find that you are more comfortable with the risks and joys of parenthood.

Taking responsibility

Each person needs to *choose* and take responsibility for having and raising the child they will produce. There's an important point here – since your partner may die, or you may split up, you have to decide to have children knowing there is a possibility that you might end up raising them alone.

Also there's another, more common pitfall – "Oh well, my partner wants a child, and is willing to do most of the work, so I will go along with it." Sorry, but it doesn't work to think this way. Fast forward a few years to when your child is a teenager, hosting a noisy party in the basement. You look at your partner with vindication and say, "Well *you* wanted the baby!"

Through exploring your own inner feelings, and those of your partner, you will learn a lot about each other, and if you decide you do want to go ahead and have a baby, then it will be with a real sense of rightness about the whole thing. You'll be far less prone to mixed feelings or partnership struggles in the early years, because you have done the preparatory soul-straightening work already. There will still be hard times, and good and bad surprises, but somewhere on the inside you will be thinking, "Yes, this is what we want to be doing!" Deep down you have a peace and strength from knowing, "We have chosen this."

There's something else it's important to remember... Our work with hundreds of families over the years has led us to believe that kids really know whether they are wanted or not. And this deep-down feeling is very different to the occasional moments all parents have when they wish their kids were in Patagonia!

It's best to not have kids if you aren't pretty sure you want them. And if you already have them, it's a good idea to commit yourself to making them welcome. Being wanted and welcome is every child's birthright.

Children are very aware of how much they are loved and wanted.

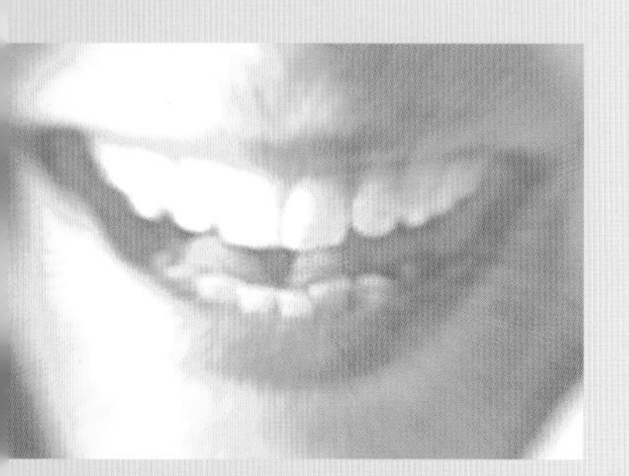

The ready or not test!

Don't you just love those questionnaires that in two minutes sort out your life's big decisions? Can they really help you? This is a lighthearted look at the multiple factors involved in deciding Your Pregnancy Potential! Tick the stars alongside the one item that best describes you.

	tick here	star rating
1 Your roles and expectations		
My partner and I are clear about sharing the workload. He/she is good with kids and wants them as much as I do		
My partner is less sure than I am about having kids		
My partner says, "Sure, we can have kids, as long as you look after them and they don't touch the stereo"...		
My partner is unsure. He/she even gets jealous of the canary		
2 Your finances		
Yes, we can afford a baby, without any real problems		
Starting a family would be a whole lot easier financially if we waited a couple more years		
We're broke all the time anyway – so what's the difference ?		
3 Your career and education		
This is a good time in my career/education to have a baby		
This is an okay time in my career/education to have a baby		
Having a baby would really disrupt my career/education		
Career? Education? Who, me?		
4 Your age		
The age I am now is the age I want to have a baby at		
I am older and I want to have a baby before time runs out		
I am young and not sure if I have the maturity to care for a baby		
I am young and there are still things I want to do..............................		
	total stars	

5 Your relationship

I have a really strong and stable relationship with my partner .... ★★★★

We have stood the test of time and we are both ready to have a child .... ★★★★

Our relationship is a bit wobbly from time to time. Maybe we should give it a little longer before starting a family .... ★★

Our relationship is shaky. Having kids will bring us closer .... ★

Relationship? Who needs it? I'll find a sperm donor somewhere .... ★

6 Your health

I've already started clearing toxins from my body, have quit smoking and stopped using any drugs. I drink very little alcohol, and have been using an alternative form of contraception to the pill for six months so its effects on my body can settle down. I'm only eating organic food. I permit no negative thoughts to enter my mind .... ★★★★

My partner is doing the same, and is staying away from workplace pollutants, farm chemicals, computer screens and petrochemical plants .... ★★★★

Some of the above .... ★★★

I'll start tomorrow .... ★

7 Your fitness

I have always been pretty fit, and am doing a gentle exercise programme which will continue during pregnancy .... ★★★★

I'll start tomorrow if it's not raining .... ★

I'm looking forward to staying home all day watching the soaps, being waited on and eating what I like .... ★

Add up all the stars that you have ticked.
If you have 20+ stars, you're probably already pregnant!
15–20 stars, you're looking pretty good.
7–15 stars, uhhh – have you considered a dog?

total stars

What will it be like?

Imagine, for a moment, that you are holding your newborn baby in your arms for the first time – carefully and tenderly. As you look down at that little face, can you feel the surge in your heartbeat? You may experience two feelings at the same time – very blessed, and very responsible. You may wonder, "Will I be a good enough parent? Will I be able to get it right?"

From the moment you discover you are pregnant, there are decisions to make. "Should I have a homebirth, or a hospital birth?"; "How soon should I stop working?" When the baby is born – "Should I ignore cries at night-time, or bring the baby into my bed?" And when you have a toddler, "How can I get them to do what they are told?"; "How old should they be before I return to work?" So many choices, so many decisions. It would be nice if somewhere, in a dusty cave, someone discovered the "Good Parenting Scrolls" – giving all the Right Answers and advice that would never fail. That would be wonderful, but it will never happen because there is no one right way – only your right way, right now, with this child.

You and your child are a unique combination, and you have to find out what works best for you both. And each child you have is different too. Searching for and finding *your* way will give you greater confidence. When people had 10 children in the families of old, they did get more confident about it. But no-one can ever be certain – you will still be soul searching when your children are long grown up.

The good news is that the wisdom you need is all around you, and inside you too. Many generations before you have raised children successfully, under all

kinds of difficult circumstances. This wisdom can still be found, in bits and pieces, shared by parents, and it helps to listen and learn. But the best guide will always be your own heart.

Learning as you go

Experience teaches you more than anything else. And certainly parenthood brings with it some remarkable experiences. You'll know what it's like to lie quietly in bed, looking at your baby's face, and feel your heart melt with a love that is beyond words. You will *also* be learning what it's like to:

- ★ change 6,800 nappies
- ★ cook and clean up after 15,000 meals
- ★ wipe snotty noses and wash little faces and hands thousands of times
- ★ put 7,800 and a half pairs of little shoes on little feet
- ★ go on hundreds of miles of walks
- ★ sit for five-and-a-half months of your life in doctors' waiting rooms
- ★ somehow (amazingly!) enjoy it all, and miss it when it's over.

No-one can really tell you in advance what parenthood feels like. It's a bit like the difference between taking a sex education class and actually making love with someone – big difference!

Your confidence in parenting develops as you do it, your inner signals subtly and gradually tell you what to do. There is a guidance system built into you, and it is not mysterious. It comes from two directions – from carefully listening to your own feelings, and from paying attention to the signals sent out by your child.

You'll be surprised at the way new abilities surface as you settle into parenthood. Loving your child means that your senses become very alert and highly developed. You start to know things without knowing how you know. We often do the right thing instinctively, given the chance. For instance, if we see a premature baby lying in a humidicrib, most of us feel an urge to reach out to it, to touch and comfort this tiny baby. We now know from

scientific studies that this impulse is right; that premature babies grow faster, gain weight and go home sooner when they are given gentle massage and touch several times each day.

Parents often have seemingly inexplicable hunches about their children's care, which turn out to be right.

“*I slept with my baby daughter in the same bed for the first three years, fearful about her restlessness and troubled breathing. People advised me not to, as it tired me out, and doctors told me there was nothing wrong with my child – that I was imagining it. All I knew was I couldn't let my baby daughter sleep alone, and that something else was not right. Eventually, at six, my daughter was diagnosed with very enlarged adenoids. She had these treated, and her sleep patterns immediately improved, and she gained weight, health and vitality.*”

Jeni, 34

Doing what's right for you

Sometimes the first job is to separate what we really think is best from the pressures and preferences of those around us.

“*I had raised four children and my husband, a doctor, had insisted that we follow “the book”, which in those days (the 40's) meant leaving children in a cot, to cry, and never cuddling or holding them for fear of spoiling. I went along with this, but when our fifth was born, a little boy, I told my husband, “This one is mine – I'm going to spoil him!” I fed the littlie in my bed, went to him if he cried, and cuddled and jiggled him on my knee as a toddler, which were all highly suspect behaviours in those days. And you know what, he's grown up to be the most well adjusted of them all!*”

Pat, 81

Learning from others

Very few of us feel equipped to be a parent when we begin. Like riding a bike, parenting is a skill, and there are tips and methods that make it easier. It is very useful to spend time around people whose parenting we admire, and from whom we can learn by imitation.

Other parents can be a great source of inspiration (as well as examples of what NOT to do!). But you don't have to be limited to the present. You have been surrounded by parenting “role models” all your life – good and bad. If you had parents who knew how to love and raise children well you are very lucky, and it will probably come easily to you too. Don't limit yourself to the same-sex parent, though. For instance, if your father was the one who taught you certain qualities, such as having fun, or being creative, you may want to incorporate his qualities into your mothering. Or as a dad, you may want to use the nurturing skills you gained from your mother. Be sure to look beyond the immediate family too – perhaps a special grandma, aunt, friendly neighbour or great schoolteacher was really good to you as a child.You might want to think of this person when you are trying to work out how to be with your own children.

Sometimes films and books portray parents who you might want to emulate. We really liked the father in the book *To Kill a Mockingbird*. There are now also some excellent parenting courses around, where good ideas are shared and where the companionship of other parents makes you feel normal and worthwhile. On the internet there are many "Parents" sites offering help and information, and lots of e-mail discussion groups where parents can natter late into the night.

I was having a lot of trouble with my strong-willed toddler, Max. However, one of my friends showed skill in disciplining Max whenever we visited her house. I was embarrassed at first, but took note of the way my friend was definite, kindly, but strong and persistent until Max co-operated. I also noticed how much Max loved to visit this friend.

So I started to use the same tone and approach that my friend had unknowingly shown me. And it started to work!

Gavin, 24

Discovering new sides to yourself

Parenthood invites you – even forces you – to extend yourself in ways you didn't think possible. Perhaps you were proudly independent as a single person. As a parent, you will get better at making friends, simply because you desperately need them! Having other mothers or fathers over to your house, or stopping to chat at the park, will give your child more chances to meet other children, and learn

Being a parent can bring out a whole new side of you.

friendship skills. This will make it easier for them when they start at playgroup or nursery.

“We moved to Australia from Scotland and had no relatives here. I was always quite shy, but I was going up the wall at home alone. I didn't know how to talk to people. I would see other mothers at the Health Centre and not know how to start. In the end, I just went up to people and said, “Hello, I'm Sue, what's your name?”, and we got talking. I started a playgroup and we have made some great friends. And guess what – my son Angus has copied me. His teacher tells me he is the most outgoing and friendly boy in the class, and really well liked.”

Sue, 32

Finding nature's way

Sometimes parenting advice may work for one person, but not another. Listen to other people, get as much information as you can, but make up your own mind. If in doubt, try something, but be ready to stop if it feels wrong. The signals from your child and your own feelings will inform you about what you should do next.

The right way will often feel easier and less forced. A common example – toilet training – features high on experts' lists, and in parents' concerns.

One woman we talked to had no idea how to approach toilet training, so she discovered her own way.

"*I had house-trained some puppies once, but that method didn't really apply! While I was trying to decide what to do, I simply let my little boy accompany me to the toilet, and bought a potty which waited hopefully in the bathroom. One day, my child came to me with the potty, and an urgent but excited look on his face. So I whipped off my little boy's nappy, and he sat on the potty and performed beautifully, and has done pretty much the same ever since. I might have been lucky, or just smart enough to read the signs. I was certainly widely envied.*"

Mara, 30

Single mothering

A number of readers will be mothers raising children on their own. Here is some extra information for you which has been learned from the many experienced single mothers we have known. (Much of this applies also to lone fathers, and there is also a section for single fathers in the Fatherhood chapter, see page 162).

★ Every parent faces almost all the same dilemmas, but the degree is different for a single parent because these dilemmas have to be faced alone. Couples raising children sometimes spend weeks just talking over what school to choose, what style of pusher to buy. They confer together on whether to take a sick child to the doctor or just wait and see. As a single parent, you have to make all these decisions on your own, and it's hard and scary.

★ On the plus side, single parenthood can be simpler, since you are not arguing or fighting over every decision or action you take. You can establish routines, feel secure through realizing you can depend on yourself, and your children can grow up to be compassionate, flexible, and resourceful people who have dealt with experiences that other children have not.

★ The attitudes of others make a big difference. There are still people who judge or blame mothers for being single, or actively discriminate against them. Yet very few mothers actually set out choosing to raise children on their own.

No-one else knows the truth about the difficult choices you have made, and the struggles that you may have gone through. Raising children is a huge job, and to succeed at it alone is an achievement to feel very proud of.

- ★ Another pressure comes from government. There seems to be a message that you should get straight back into the workplace and be "productive". Yet you may feel that your children, especially if they are very young, need you MORE because you are their only parent, and the risk is that they will get even less of you because of the pressure to return to work.
- ★ Kids need us to be involved in their lives, but not so involved that our whole life is wrapped up in theirs. With single parenthood there is more of a risk that your child can come to be the focus of all your energies to an unhealthy degree. Or it can go the other way, and you can be so busy just coping, that they come to feel you are unavailable and they cannot bother you with their feelings and fears. You need to have adult friends who can help you keep a balanced perspective.
- ★ You need to stay healthy, eat well, exercise, and learn to relax. Have at least some time for yourself each day. It's tempting to become a martyr and rush about becoming stressed, but this can lead to further problems that take even longer to sort out (like losing the keys to your front door!).
- ★ Do whatever you can to help keep your child's father involved in their life. Be creative and co-operative as much as you can. Keep trying for a workable arrangement. Your child needs to be able to love you both. Help your child to have contact with carefully selected, trustworthy and good men (grandfather, uncle, cousin, teacher, sports coach).
- ★ All parents need community. Look for a living situation which is "people rich" – close to families with whom you can jointly invest in each other's children and lives. Through the school, church, social clubs, yoga or gym, you will build more fun and support for yourself and have role models for your children. Joining parenting courses or support groups means you can talk over concerns and get reinforcement.

How parenthood heals you too

It's often easy to think that your children are the only ones benefiting from all your hard work – that the "giving" is all one way. But parenthood is really a two-way flow of learning and growth between parent and child. You don't need to spend very long in the company of a child before you start to feel as if you are being dismantled and rebuilt. And, in fact, that's just what is happening. That the strong emotional reactions you sometimes have, the intense feelings and times of confusion or turmoil, all indicate that you are changing as a person, and healing your personal history too.

The way that this works is very simple. As your child passes through each stage of growing up, you too will revisit the needs and issues of that stage. This is natural and automatic, and it happens for fathers as well as mothers. Here's an instance – as you cradle your new baby and tend to their needs you are also feeling empathically what it is like to *be* a baby; to be held and loved, kept warm and fed and comforted. People often experience this sense of deep satisfaction in giving love to a baby. You are unknowingly nurturing yourself as you are nurturing your child. If you didn't get enough care as a baby, you may feel a special sense of healing in giving your baby what you would have liked to receive.

The process of revisiting your childhood as you grow as a parent can, of course, be painful and, at these times, when you feel inadequate or even distressed, it's important to attend to healing yourself so that you can fulfil your child's needs. This next story is a very typical instance of this...

"*I loved my two children dearly, but found it hard to show them any affection. When I watched other mothers hugging and smooching their babies and toddlers, I felt awkward and tense because I couldn't do this with my children. One day, walking home after talking with a close friend, I realized that I couldn't remember ever being held or comforted by my own*

You will feel a special sense of healing as you give your baby the care you would like to have received.

mother. A sudden rush of tears came to my eyes. Remembering the loneliness of my own childhood, I began finding it easier to be close to my kids, and to my husband. It didn't happen overnight, and took some courage, as I softened my tough outer shell to be in touch with how lonely I really felt. But my capacity for closeness slowly increased, and I felt happier than ever before. As a bonus, my kids seemed happier, had fewer behaviour problems than before, and my marriage grew stronger. ”

Margaret, 52

Often today, a man who didn't know his own father, or was never very close to him, can feel the joy of being able to change this pattern with his own children, helping them to trust him and know him more closely. Parenthood can help you to heal hurts which have come down through many generations.

The empathy you feel for your child can guide you in what to do when a nurturing response is needed, or even when discipline is called for. As you confront your toddler, eyeball to eyeball, across the pieces of broken crockery on the kitchen floor, it helps to remember the frustrations of being little and clumsy, and the shame of being blamed as a child. Perhaps you will be gentler, less likely to overreact.

Perhaps when you were a child, your parents lost control and hit you angrily. You remember clearly how scary this felt. Armed with this awareness, you make a clear decision to control your actions when you are feeling angry. As a result of this, your children can always feel safe around you. What a wonderful outcome this is – all resulting from your ability to empathize and remember being a little child.

Is parenting worth it?

Have you ever met or heard of someone who is a really wonderful human being? They have come through tough times, they are kind, strong, funny, gracious and sparkle with life. Parenthood, if you stick with it, and if you are lucky enough to get the support you need, can turn you into this kind of person.

There is an exquisite, powerful and healing connection between every parent and child. Every caring action you make, large or small, contributes to your own wellbeing and that of your child.

The "special moments" with a child are great, but just as vital are the routine times, the little corrections to behaviour, the assistance you give, explanations, comforts and directions. All these everyday things add up to helping your child become a fully alive, loving and capable adult.

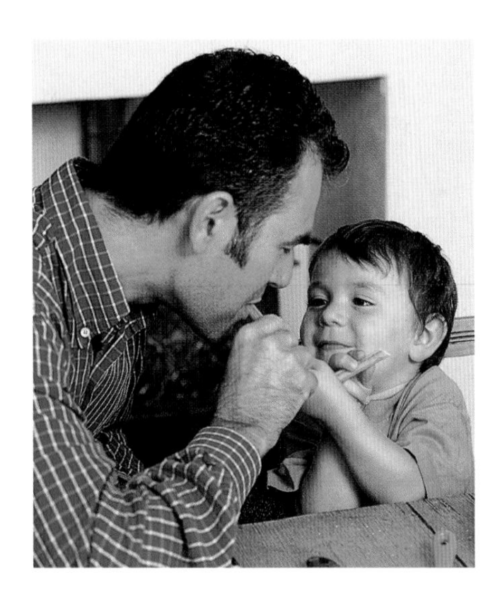

The "special moments" are great, but just as vital are the routine times.

As a parent, many things are required of you – practical skills, understanding and resourcefulness. You are the key person though. You are at the heart of the process. Your kids may not learn to be loving unless you show them love and encourage them. They may not learn to solve problems, unless you help them to think clearly, and to understand their own feelings. You have the chance to make them healthy as you teach them to like good food and take joy in using their bodies actively.

Loving, alert, healthy children don't just happen. The seed is there – children love to love, they love to explore, learn, eat, exercise, be creative. But these things need to be drawn out, nurtured and taught. Luckily, it isn't all up to you. You and your child are two souls meeting. Your child brings a unique disposition, health, handicaps and talents. You bring all of your background, life experiences and imperfections. (Your partner,

your other children, friends, family and community all add to the melting pot of experiences!) In the same way that our body sucks vitamins out of the food we eat, children get what they need from every person who is around them. Even the people they *don't* like teach them lessons about life.

> "*Loving, alert, healthy children don't just happen. The seed is there ... but these things need to be drawn out, nurtured and taught.*"

Without wanting to scare you, let us say that parenting is a huge thing. Raising kids is more significant in terms of affecting the lives of other human beings than anything else most of us will ever do. How you raise your children will affect all their relationships. The qualities they possess or lack will affect all the people they ever meet, learn from and work with, especially those they love and live with, and the children they raise, and *their* children, for ever after.

This is the big view, something to remember when you can't see the wood for the trees (or the child for the nappies!). In an 80-year life, you are spending a few years helping a child get started. We are willing to bet that when you are old and grey, it's these "precious years" that will give you the most pleasure to look back on.

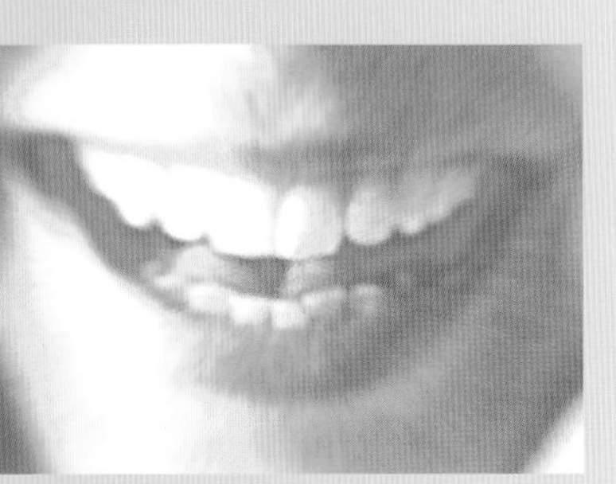

Parenting... you just have to smile

Parents have a unique sense of humour – earthy, rather dark, and slightly hysterical. Here is some popular internet advice on "Preparing for parenthood".

for starters

Go to the local chemist, tip the contents of your wallet onto the counter and tell the pharmacist to help him/herself.

Then go to the supermarket. Arrange to have your wages paid directly to their head office. Go home. On the way pick up a paper and read it for the last time.

Next, put on a dressing gown and stick a beanbag down the front. Leave it there for nine months. After nine months take out 10 per cent of the beans.

riding in the car

Forget the car and buy a minivan.

Buy a chocolate icecream and put it in the glove compartment.

Leave it there.

Get a coin and stick it in the cassette player. Take a family size packet of chocolate biscuits and mash them down the back seats. Run a garden rake along both sides of the vehicle.

goodbye to nights

To see how the nights will feel, walk around the living room from 5pm to 10pm carrying a wet bag weighing about 8–12 lb. At 10pm put the bag down, set the alarm for midnight and go to sleep. Get up at 12am and walk around the room again with the bag until 1am. Put the alarm on for 3am. As you can't get back to sleep, get up at 2am and make a drink. Go to bed at 2.45am. Get up again at 3am when the alarm goes off. Sing songs in the dark until 4am. Put the alarm on for 5am. Get up. Make breakfast. Look cheerful.

table manners

Hollow out a melon and make a small hole in the side. Suspend it from the ceiling and swing it from side to side.

Get a bowl of soggy cereal and attempt to spoon it into the swinging melon while making aeroplane noises. Continue until half the cereal is gone. Tip the rest into your lap, making sure that a lot falls down your legs and onto the floor.

leaving promptly!

Get ready to go out. Wait outside the toilet for half an hour. Go out the front door. Come in again. Go out. Walk down the front path. Walk back up it. Walk down it again. Walk very slowly down the road for five minutes. Stop to inspect minutely every cigarette end, piece of used chewing gum, dirty tissue and dead insect along the way. Retrace your steps. Scream that you can't stand it any more, until the neighbours come out and stare at you. You are now just about ready to try taking a small child for a walk.

having all the answers

Find a couple who are already parents and berate them about their methods of discipline, lack of patience, appallingly low tolerence levels and how they have allowed their children to run riot.

Suggest ways in which they might improve their child's sleeping habits, toilet training, table manners and overall behaviour. Enjoy it – it'll be the last time you'll have all the answers.

shopping for fun and relaxation

Go to your local supermarket. Take with you the nearest thing you can find to a pre-school child – a fully-grown goat is excellent. If you intend to have more than one child, take more than one goat. Do your week's shopping without letting the goats out of your sight. Pay for everything the goats eat or destroy.

hygiene

Smear peanut butter on the sofa and jam onto the curtains. Hide a fish finger behind the stereo and leave it there all summer. Stick your fingers in the flowerbeds, then rub them on the clean walls. Cover the stains with crayon.

dressing small children

First, buy an octopus and a string bag. Attempt to put the octopus into the string bag so that none of the arms hang out. Time allowed for this – all morning.

chapter 2

pregnancy and birth-the inside story

Your feelings in pregnancy

Pregnancy is a little like catching a wave. From the very second that new life is conceived inside you, powerful hormonal forces are unleashed to carry you successfully through. You are still the one doing the steering, but there is a "Wow! Whoosh! Lookout!" kind of quality to it all as you ride the wave of changes that are sweeping through you.

Even before conception, once you've decided you want to get pregnant, things begin to happen. Many women find that they feel a new and different kind of pleasure in their love-making. There is often a strong feeling of rightness, purpose, excitement and joy. It's a time of feeling more open-hearted and closer to your partner.

Conception

Some women report knowing the exact moment they have conceived. Many others "know" they are pregnant before any test has been done. How do they know? There seems to be a combination of intuition and sensitivity to body changes that helps a woman to notice the very earliest stirrings of the new life beginning inside. For those of us who are not so intuitive, pregnancy test kits (available without prescription from any pharmacy) can tell you in minutes if you are pregnant!

Whether it has taken a long or short time for you to conceive, whether planned or unplanned, feared or hoped for, the moment of confirmation of pregnancy is an awesome event, deserving of celebration. Congratulations! Go out for a special meal (with mineral water – damn!).

Getting over the shock!

Even if all the preamble has been positive, the momentous realization of definitely being pregnant is still accompanied by just plain *shock*! Parents find themselves thinking "Not yet – I'm not ready", at the same time as (and perhaps because of) knowing they can't go back. Even the most longed-for, hoped-for and awaited pregnancy still does not escape this "Oh my God" reaction.

What you are really feeling, at these times, is the truth that is always there, which we choose to ignore most of the time – that nature, or God, or the power of the universe, runs our lives. We are never in complete control. You are on the roller coaster and it just pulled out of the station! Whenever we are passing through these big life transitions, it is very good for us to realize that we can "want what we want" with all our hearts, we can make our plans so carefully, but in the end it's nature that chooses. So don't feel scared. Let yourself breathe just a little deeper and slower, expand your spirit and feel what it really is – not fear, but awe. You are in on the creation of life.

> *"Even the most longed-for, hoped-for and awaited pregnancy does not escape this 'Oh my God' reaction."*

Perhaps the first and most important realization of parenthood is that we provide the raw materials, make our bodies, hearts and minds available to parenting, and wait for life to fill in the space when and as it wills. This same lesson is repeated in the pregnancy, the birth, the child's growing years, adolescence, adulthood, and even on to death.

We can only do our best. It's tough, but very helpful to realize that we can't control life – we can only dance with it. The reality is that children can die or be born disabled, we or our partner may be hurt or injured. Nothing in life is certain. We have inner resources that we have never tapped and so have our friends and family around us. We can be careful, but we must also learn to not worry, to trust ourselves and the forces of life to carry us through.

Good things to try

Pregnancy diary

You can buy or make a daily diary for your pregnancy. This gives you the opportunity to jot down a little note about what you are experiencing and doing each day.
Be practical as well as reflective, it will help you to get your thoughts clear...

- ★ ***For example, you might note down visits to the doctor or midwife***: questions you asked, the answers you received and your feelings about these, and questions you want to ask at your next visit.
- ★ ***Important moments can be recorded:*** the pregnancy test, hearing the baby's heartbeat, the first kicks, and so on. This makes fascinating reading for your child in later years and is amazing to re-read especially in subsequent pregnancies for comparison. In the blurry time of pregnancy, you will have kept precious memories to enjoy later. Writing a diary focuses you and gives you a sense of your own personal growth while measuring your progress towards the time of the birth.
- ★ ***A father might also choose to write a letter to his unborn child***: in it he can talk about his own life so far, his childhood and parents, and the life he now lives as he waits for the child's arrival. In it he can share his feelings and hopes. By reflecting and writing down these thoughts, he will become more aware and fascinated by his own changes. Perhaps one day he will give the letter to his own son or daughter as they too prepare for impending parenthood.

Why pregnancy takes nine months

You may think pregnancy is a time when your body grows a little baby, and that's all. However, it is so much more than this. Pregnancy is the time when YOU change – making one of the biggest shifts in your whole life cycle. Just as puberty changed you forever from a child to a young adult, pregnancy changes you into someone utterly new. You are being readied for a phase of your life so different that every aspect of you is being transformed. Just as adolescents sometimes wish they could go back to being a child, you may fight this change at first, but soon come to embrace and enjoy your new self as being so much richer and more interesting than the old.

Both men and women undergo these life transitions, but with varying degrees of support. In older societies, such transitions were clearly marked, helped and celebrated. For us though, the rituals have disappeared, and the helpful interventions of others have been weakened or lost entirely. We are no longer handed the key to the door at 21 (some of us got that at age seven!). We might have an 18th birthday party or celebrate 16 as the big shift to adulthood – no-one is quite sure any more. Legal rights and responsibilities, like driving a car, sexual consent, voting, earning a living, appear at various times spread over this period, so you are never quite sure whether you have "arrived" as an adult.

Your first pregnancy, though, is an undeniable change. You may be moving from girl to woman, and at the same time from woman to mother. Boy becomes man becomes father. Pregnancy is the beginning of a stage of life which can make you a wiser, stronger and (in every sense!) more rounded human being.

Good things to try

Getting ready for bonding

During pregnancy, you will find yourselves daydreaming and fantasizing about what sort of child you will have. This is an important part of preparing yourself for your baby's arrival. You can try this now. In your imagination, think of your child and just let the answers come to you...

* *Will you have a boy or a girl?*
* *What colour eyes and hair will the baby have?*
* *Will the baby be like you in looks or personality?*
* *How will you all get along and where will this baby fit in with other children, existing or planned?*
* *What will you do together? How will your time be spent?*
* *How will your partner relate to the baby?*
* *What kind of things will you enjoy doing?*
* *Which parts will be hard and challenging?*
* *What will the child be like as a schoolchild, teenager and adult?*
* *What, especially, are you looking forward to?*

These are some of the thoughts and questions which help to make a space in our lives, beginning the natural and vital process which is often called bonding or attachment. The reality may differ from the fantasy, but it is good to prime your mind and heart by thinking in this way, and bringing unconscious hopes and dreams to the surface.

"Children come in all shapes and sizes and you'll never be sure what you're going to get!"

The nine-month transition

The early years of your child's life will go so much better if your mind and spirit have had time to prepare, to think and plan – time to develop a deep reserve of restfulness and purpose. Parents who have to continue a stressful job, or throw themselves into frenetic housework or other projects, can find themselves suddenly in the labour ward or at home with a new baby having enormous emotional turmoil. It's as if you had suddenly arrived at some distant destination without any chance to pack, plan or think, or even noticed you were travelling.

The nine months it takes for your body to make a baby are a gift to you because you need every second. Not to rush or worry, but the complete opposite – to contemplate the new you that is emerging, to let go of the old self that had different priorities. And to make room for this new, small person in your life. Your baby is being born, and you are being reborn. These changes are huge, and the waiting is preparation time that lets you get used to the whole idea.

Your body and heart will send you clear signals about how to make this transition. If, during your pregnancy, you have a sense of being too busy, rushed or bothered, then take notice of this. Stop, and make time. Realize that something important is going on, and you could miss it if you skim over it with busy-ness and outward looking concerns. Whether you are the mother- or the father-to-be, realize that a process is happening on the inside. You may find yourself taking long walks, sitting meditatively gazing at the sky or having powerful dreams.

In whatever way suits you, find the enjoyment in your pregnancy – quiet contemplation, yoga or health projects, reading inspiring books, listening to glorious music, or just stroking your pregnant tummy and watching it grow.

If this is not your first child

A second or third pregnancy is no less significant, and brings its own special adjustments. This is the time in which you begin to get used to yourself as a parent of a larger family.

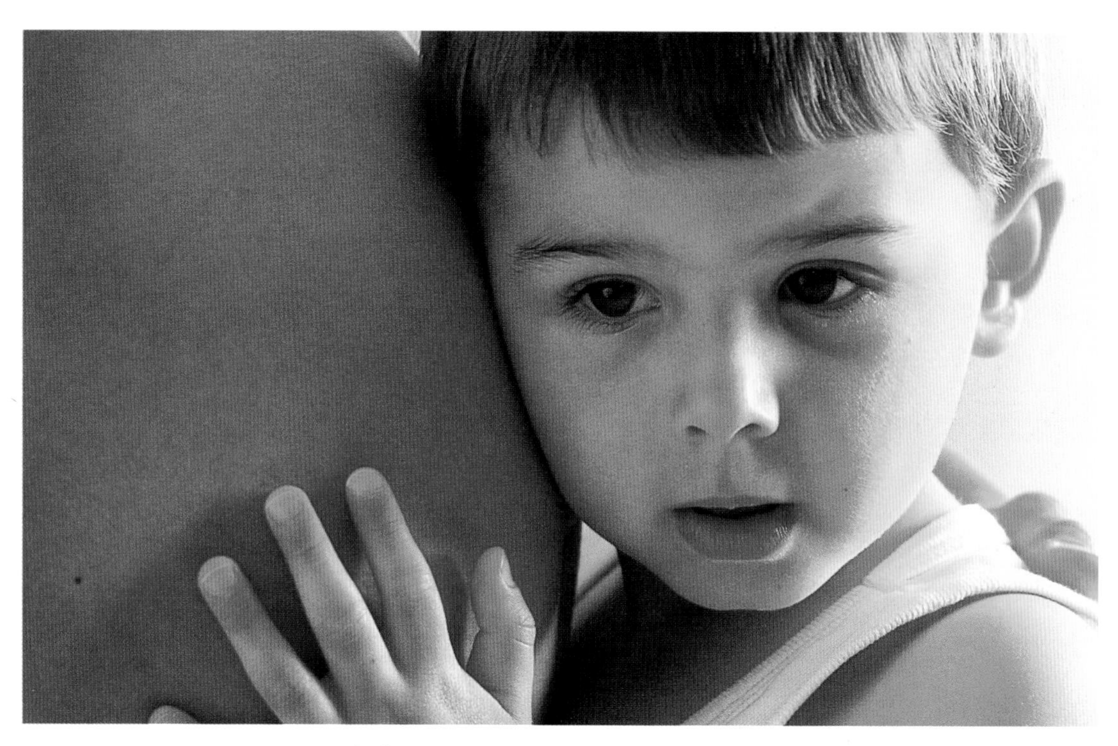

"During my second pregnancy, I started having this nightmare where I couldn't find my first child in a burning house. My mother reassured me that, in her view, this was just because I was adjusting to the idea of a new baby, and that made a lot of sense. I was panicking, thinking 'I've given so much to this first child, how could I begin with a new child and have enough left over?' I relaxed somewhat, and haven't had that dream again. With three children now, I have found that it somehow works out."

Sandi, 32

This is also an important adjustment time for the other children in the family, who are about to have a new baby brother or sister. Seeing mum's belly swelling up or feeling the baby kick helps them get used to the idea of a new family member on the way. There is a lot to get used to – the youngest will lose their place as the youngest, which they might have been enjoying! Everyone will have to "move up". This may be why new parents often choose to have a gift ready to give their children "from the baby", after it is born. It is a symbolic offering – of the future gifts it brings.

Riding out emotional storms

People tend to dismiss the intense feelings of parents-to-be as "just hormones" or "getting emotional". Yet what could be more emotional – or beautiful – than growing a new human being. Pregnancy brings the full range of feelings – from satisfaction, contentment, serenity, pride, joy, gratitude, through to the challenging feelings of fear, confusion, irritation and all shades of anger.

The pain of miscarriage

Pete and Janet experienced a miscarriage during their first pregnancy. People don't talk much about miscarriage, yet as many as one in five pregnancies end in this sad way. The emotional pain is often underestimated and it can influence feelings in subsequent pregnancies.

"*I was sad for many months and it was hard to find friends to talk about it. I had to return to work the very next day, and it was only many months later that I broke through my defences and cried while talking to some close friends who listened and gave me the support I needed.*"

Pete, 25

"*I was amazed how the loss of our first baby came up again when we got pregnant for a second time. I knew in my rational part that things were going well, that there was no special need to worry. But I found I was so alert to any signs of cramping, pain, stress, etc, that reminded me of the miscarriage. A mild attack of cramps (when I was 14 weeks pregnant) came when I was at work. They passed without any consequence, but when I got home, I was immediately filled with memories of the night when I had lost my first baby, and I cried for a long time. Pete just held me and he was really understanding. While I had been sad at the time of the miscarriage, I guess there had been deeper sadness which I hadn't allowed myself to feel. After that night, I felt a lot more relaxed and less afraid to love this new baby.*"

Janet, 23

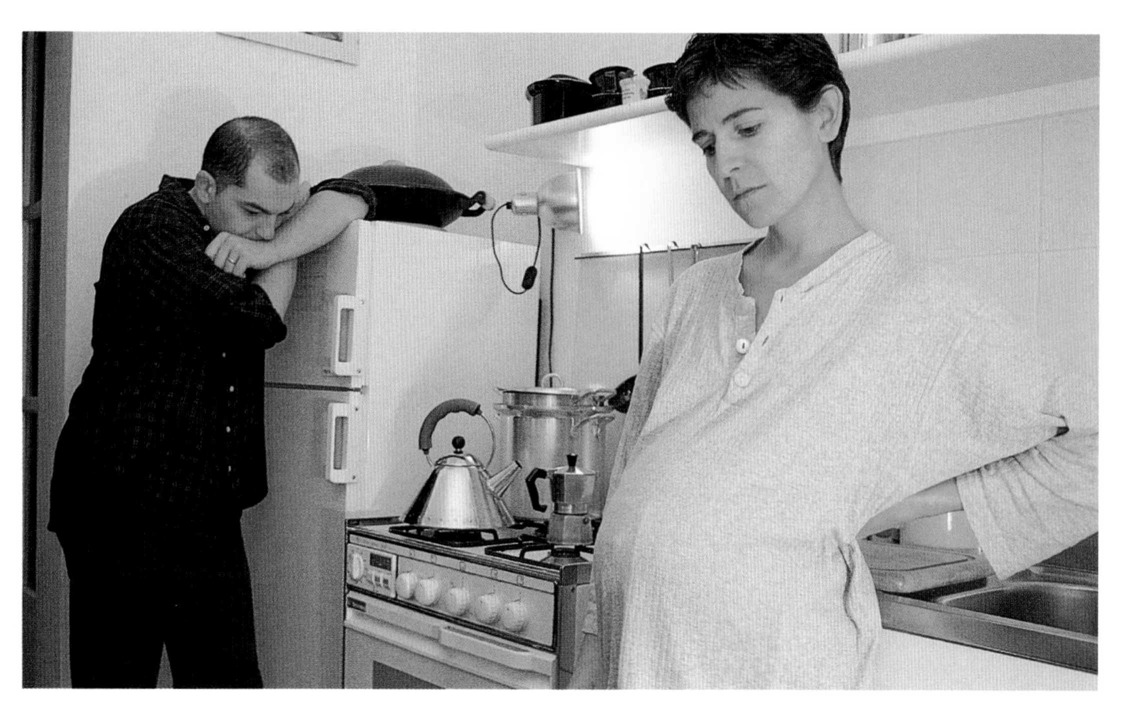

Overcoming fears

The early months of pregnancy are vulnerable ones for many of us. It is helpful to notice, write down or talk about any fears and worries, no matter how illogical they may seem. Seemingly out of nowhere, concerns will often surface about the birth process, your ability to handle the responsibilities, your fears for your child's future.

During pregnancy and right into labour, our emotions are very open. Sometimes whole pieces of our past come tumbling out, in a kind of psychic spring cleaning which can be unsettling until we figure them out, let go of them and move on.

“*My labour was not proceeding properly, and there was a lull while the health staff considered what to do. An older nurse took a moment or two to sit with me and ask me how I was feeling. All at once I began to sob and repeat something about, 'I don't want to lose it.' Rather than offer a bland reassurance, the nurse asked what I meant. I tearfully told the nurse about a baby I had given birth to when I was only 14. The baby had been taken from me and given away for adoption, never seen or touched by me. I had put this to the back of my mind, as much as I could, but now the pain of that old loss was preventing me releasing this baby into the world. The nurse gave me a clear commitment that this baby would not be taken away. In a short time my contractions began strongly again and I gave birth to a 7lb boy who was immediately placed in my joyful arms.* ”

Marina, 27

Although Marina's story is unusually intense, we have met many parents-to-be who have, in the course of pregnancy, had to release leftover feelings from:

★ termination (abortion) experiences
★ earlier births which have been difficult or mishandled
★ caesarean operations which took away some of the early connection with a baby
★ previous separations from a newborn for medical reasons, warranted or unwarranted
★ experiences of rape or sexual abuse.

Good things to try

Activity and your emotions

For a mother-to-be, the overall guideline for all feelings in pregnancy is that you are making space – not just in your body, but in your mind too. And the way to make space is to clear out the junk. So express yourself!

★ ***If you feel the need***, go into a room and make all the gruesome noises you can manage. Beat up a mattress with a rolled-up towel if you want to.
★ ***It's alright to feel bad and let go.*** This will make room for relaxation, excitement and quiet joy to creep into the spaces you have made.
★ ***Whenever you are depressed*** or feeling stuck, the key to helping your mind is to move your body. Get up, get dressed, go out. Do exercise – even just the shortest imaginable walk down the street and back – and notice how it makes you feel better.
★ ***Try dancing, swimming or yoga.*** Men, please give your partner encouragement and gratitude. What she eats, how she exercises, takes care of herself and her body is also for the benefit of your baby. Never nag, but do reward like crazy.
★ ***Remember – this is a temporary state.*** You won't be pregnant for the rest of your life! The effort is worth it. One day soon you will have a little, soft-skinned, tender baby in your arms. Imagine this often – both of you healthy, relaxed, loving, happy and content.

Once these feelings have been understood, you can take any action that is needed, and express any feelings that have waited a chance to release. You can emerge a freer and more empowered person and this can be one of the gifts of your pregnancy.

Having said this, the perspective is important. Most women come to childbirth with relative serenity and things go smoothly and well. And not all fears are because of the past. A lot of it is just practical – you need knowledge about a subject that you have had little to do with before. Knowledge is power – if you don't know your vernix from your perineum, then you should find out! Book into good antenatal classes, visit local hospitals and birthing centres, talk to hospital and homebirth midwives. There are many great books on the specifics of birth.

Fears are always best allayed by taking action to make things the way you want them to be. You may find yourself suddenly realizing that you want to:

* work out with your partner the type of support you want at the birth
* be more active in seeking out a really compatible doctor, a better hospital, a good midwife
* know more about your own body, your rights and your personal preferences.

I'm NOT Happy!!

Anger is another emotion familiar to most pregnant women. The first three months (when morning sickness is common) provide some reasons to feel annoyed! You are surrounded by people saying "How wonderful, congratulations, you must be so excited", and all you can feel is seasick!

There's another aspect too – something outside your control is taking over! We call it the "Move Over, There's Two of Us in This Body" phase. The plus side of this is a delightful feeling of company – a little presence that is now always with you wherever you go. Morning sickness is a reminder that it's all really happening. But what a reminder! You may also be experiencing some of the following:

★ pressure on your bladder, which turns your shopping trips into toilet tours
★ sore breasts
★ bowel changes and digestion difficulties
★ a general and sharp increase in sensitivity.

The biggest sensitivity change is probably towards smells. Cooking smells can make you feel dreadful, so can fish smells, or strong perfumes – all can send you dashing out for fresh air. Exhaust fumes, petrol and cigarette smoke can all be irritating. And for good reason – they are bad for you and your baby.

Many women also report greater sensitivity to outside influences, such as feeling more affected by television programmes and more distressed by news items, especially those about children. They are also open to other people's advice, and affected by negative birth stories which people gratuitously seem to want to share. So stay around more positive people, and perhaps give the news a miss for the duration of your pregnancy. You won't miss much – and it isn't the real world anyway, just the collected disasters! You and the new life inside you are the real world.

Explain your feelings to each other and be compassionate.

Remember, your anger is alerting you to the need for changes – so go ahead and make them. As with the fears, let people know what you don't and do want. You are pregnant – enjoy throwing your weight around!

Feeling like sex, or not?

Many women feel healthy, sexy and full of energy, but sometimes during pregnancy a woman's libido drops through the floor. Often this is just hormonal. But also it's hard to feel sexy or romantic when you feel like you've been seasick since the beginning of time. This can be discouraging for your partner, so it's important to explain your feelings to each other and be compassionate. Many couples begin a process of finding other ways to give pleasure and reassurance other than their usual patterns of intercourse.

Some men feel cautious about hurting the baby or starting labour, and are happier with other ways of being sexual – enjoy the changes and variety. Some men are less attracted to a pregnant spouse, while others find their partner especially attractive. The main issue is to be considerate. If sex was just something routine you took for granted, then you'll learn something new – that sensitivity and giving and winning a partner's affections are what make lovemaking deeper and more satisfying in the long run. This is a chance to broaden the number of ways you show your caring for each other.

Good things to try

Three-way care

Pregnancy suddenly means you have multiple responsibilities – to yourself, to your baby and to your partnership (if you have one). It's a new juggling act, but not an impossible one. Maintaining a balance – caring for baby/self/partner – will bring harmony during pregnancy and afterwards as a new family.

Care of your baby

You may be tough, but your baby isn't. So you need to eat really well, avoid cigarettes, drugs, alcohol, certain medications, fumes, chemicals, sprays and paints. Your doctor can advise you about other hazards to avoid. And, of course, research, as well as common sense, recommends staying out of highly stressed work or other situations.

Care of yourself

Includes being kind to yourself, listening to what your body wants (it will often tell you). For instance:

★ ***if you are feeling tired, stop and rest (yes, we know, pretty obvious – so do it!)***
★ ***if you are feeling hemmed-in or depressed, exercise, walk, go out and visit a friend***
★ ***if you are feeling scared, angry or sad, talk it over, look for help from others. Find out what you need to feel calm again.***

Care of your partnership

This means that in preparing for the birth you don't stop doing things you enjoy. Give lots of praise to each other. Confide in each other first, rather than other people (but do keep up friendships and family support too). Visit the doctor and hospital and birth classes together. Do nice things for each other out of the blue. Enjoy some evenings out, and treat these as special – partly since these occasions are an endangered species now!

> *I just never felt like sex while I was pregnant. I didn't like my own body, or how it felt, and Rob's attentions just made me feel worse. One evening though, he was less pushy, but didn't go off in a huff either. He just gave me a very slow, gentle, strong back massage, and I started to feel glad I did have a body, and I felt less like a sack of potatoes. I felt relieved and cared for, and was surprised at the extra energy and interest that were released in me to also care for him.*
>
> *Sandy, 32*

A note for fathers

You can be a huge amount of help during the pregnancy. Encourage your partner, who is, after all, doing the heavy work! Encourage her to walk with you when she feels sluggish or "stuck". Foot massages and backrubs are very much appreciated. Buy loads of really nourishing groceries and stock the kitchen. Get into a routine of sharing cooking, shopping, washing, cleaning up and ironing. In the last month of pregnancy, cook or make arrangements to prepare meals that you can freeze, ready for after your baby is born.

There's an in-built danger here, because the stage of life when you are a prospective father is often the time that you are most worried about your job, perhaps working longer hours to get advancement at work. Many men have an almost hormonal burst of provider-fever at this time and feel they have to renovate the house, or buy a bigger one, so asking you to cook meals and get home early might sound a little unfair. But, actually, some of the grand plans are better delayed. Your time, and a little relaxation, are more important in building caring and enjoyment into the pregnancy and early months with your child. If you start to remodel the kitchen, your partner will probably feel guilty and start regrouting the bathroom, just to prove she is pulling her weight. Better to both work on making life simple and easy.

The way our society is organized doesn't help. One day soon we hope to see, as normal and accepted, laws guaranteeing parental leave, and shorter working hours for young fathers and mothers.

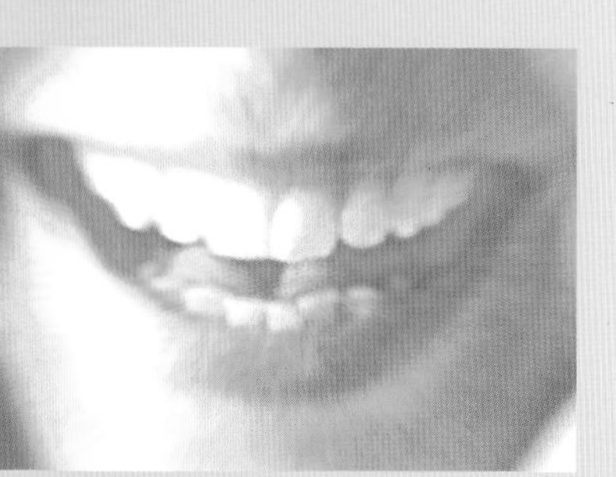

Pregnancy... you just have to smile

Parents of small children go through many personality changes. Perhaps the most notable is the development of a slightly hysterical sense of humour. This may be our most powerful survival tool! Here is some pregnancy-related humour to get you started.

Q Am I more likely to get pregnant if my husband wears boxer shorts rather than briefs?

A Yes, but you'll have an even better chance if he doesn't wear anything at all.

Q My brother tells me that since my husband has a big nose, and genes for big noses are dominant, my baby will have a big nose as well. Is this true?

A The odds are greater that your brother will have a fat lip.

Q What is the easiest way to figure out exactly when I got pregnant?

A Have sex once a year.

Q My husband and I are very attractive. I'm sure our baby will be beautiful enough for commercials. Whom should I contact about this?

A Your therapist.

Q What is the most common pregnancy craving?

A For men to be the ones who get pregnant.

Q My blood type is O-positive and my husband's is A-negative. What if my baby is born, say, type AB-positive?

A Then the game is up.

Q **I'm two months pregnant now. When will my baby move?**

A With any luck, right after he finishes university.

Q **How will I know if my vomiting is morning sickness or the flu?**

A If it's the flu, you'll get better.

Q **Ever since I've been pregnant, I haven't been able to go to bed at night without onion rings. Is this a normal craving?**

A Depends on what you're doing with them.

Q **Since I became pregnant, my breasts, rear end, and even my feet have grown. Is there anything that gets smaller during pregnancy?**

A Yes, your bladder.

Q **The more pregnant I get, the more often strangers smile at me. Why?**

A Cause you're fatter than they are.

Q **Will I love my dog less when the baby is born?**

A No, but your husband might get on your nerves.

Q **My wife is five months pregnant and so moody that sometimes she's almost irrational.**

A So what's your question, goatface?

Q **Under what circumstances can sex at the end of pregnancy bring on labour?**

A When the sex is between your husband and another woman.

The birth experience

During your pregnancy you will get to know your birthing options. You may want to visit maternity hospitals in your area, talk to homebirth midwives or seek out a birthing centre. Usually your GP will give you regular check-ups and in some countries they will also refer you to a specialist obstetrician. It's a good idea for both partners to go to these appointments, taking with them a list of questions in case they feel too rushed to remember everything they wanted to ask. Always seek out a doctor, obstetrician, hospital and midwife that you feel comfortable and happy with – ask other people their recommendations. With a good medical carer, you will feel you can ask questions and you are answered clearly and not talked down to. This sense of confidence will help you to relax and feel like an equal, so you will feel more empowered and less self-conscious in the process of birthing.

"Expect that you will have a safe and normal delivery. But also be ready to accept that things might not go strictly to plan and this can still be okay."

A partner or midwife helps the birth along with massage, coaching in breathing techniques and giving support. If you are not at home for the birth, try to get that "at home" feeling by taking comfortable slippers, a special photo, shawl or favourite music to the birthing place, or having trusted support people available and involved.

Be optimistic. Expect that you will have a safe and normal delivery. But also be ready to accept that things might not go strictly to plan and this can still be okay. Mothers, use your partner and friends to ask questions, be assertive and look after your welfare.

Photographs are essential. Have lots of film, two cameras or even a camcorder. It's great if someone else can take some photos, then the father can enter into the process more fully

– he could have his hands full at the time! Whatever kind of birth you have, you will want to revisit those never-to-be-relived moments (and so will your child).

Story of a birth

What will your birth be like? No two experiences are alike. Here we let a first-time mother, ***Diane Mallett***, recount the experience of the birth of her daughter.

“*For my husband, Ian, and myself, the birth of our daughter Amy was perhaps the most dramatic and impressive event of our lives, although, medically speaking, it was routine and unremarkable. So much goes into making up the event covered by the words 'birth experience' that it is difficult to know where to begin and end. It is like sorting through old photographs, trying to decide which images are both significant and relevant. I should begin by saying*

I am a trained nurse and midwife, since that coloured so much of the experience for me. I had delivered dozens of babies, but all my working hours were put in prior to giving birth myself. How differently I see everything now, having lived through the labour and delivery of my own child! As a nurse, I tried to empathize with my patients, but there is no way of appreciating the pain of labour or the joy which makes it all worthwhile until one has been through it. When I think of the advice I gave women in labour – 'Remember your exercises', 'Breathe deeply and the pain will ease', 'Just relax' – I realize that, although the words were sincerely meant and seemed appropriate at the time, they appear mere platitudes in retrospect.

Ian and I were thrilled by our pregnancy. Though I was familiar with the information handed out in antenatal and parenthood classes, we were happy to receive instruction at our local hospital in order to get into the spirit of the coming event and feel fully prepared for it as a couple. So much depends on attitude and I was determined to have a casebook pregnancy and labour, not to mention a casebook baby.

I am an organized person and used to wonder how women could be unsure of their dates, but my doctor, the ultrasound and I came up with three different due dates, none of which proved very accurate in the event. A visit to my doctor in early May assured me I would not be going into labour for several weeks, as the baby's head had not dropped. Ian and I decided on a weekend at the coast, several hours' drive from home. After a day of walking miles along the beach, we went out to dinner, had a good night's sleep and, at 10 am the following morning, my membranes ruptured.

I had explained this event to many women but, when it happened to me, I was incredulous. I had assumed I would go into gentle labour, spend several hours resting at home, then go to hospital only when I was about to go into second stage. Now I needed to be admitted to hospital as soon as possible. Since the baby's head was not engaged, there was a possibility of the cord prolapsing and encircling the neck. I felt surprised, disappointed and upset. I also felt debilitated by the water flowing from me uncontrollably.

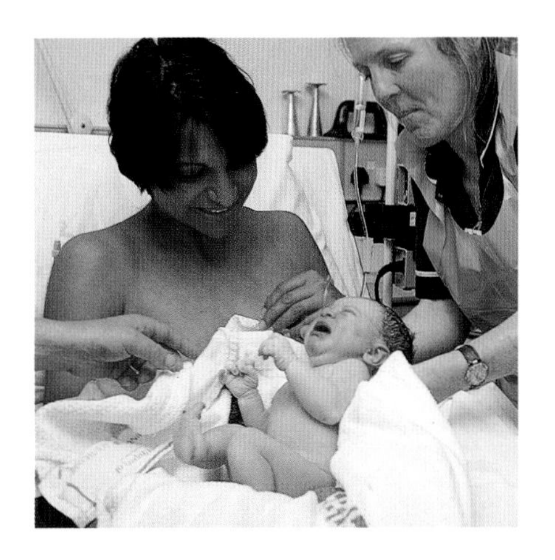

Contractions began soon after the membranes ruptured and we bundled into the car to begin the three-hour drive to hospital. I timed my contractions, while Ian cursed caravans slowing our journey. We thought of the hospitals en route, in case I did the unlikely with our first and gave birth rapidly. I kept wondering if there could be another explanation for the flow of amber liquid, if we would feel foolish for cutting short an enjoyable weekend for a false alarm, but I knew in my mind this must be it.

Even when one feels prepared for an event and happily anticipates it, the reality can come as a shock. I was admitted to the labour ward by a sister who said 'poor thing' when I told her my membranes had ruptured – sympathy in advance for the long wait I would probably have in hospital. Contractions had all but ceased by this time and I felt that my doctor might do an induction in a couple of days' time, if no progress was made. I was not keen for this type of intervention and my doctor had assured me he would not implememt any treatment I was not happy with. But, at the same time, I was not prepared to put the baby at risk just for the sake of going into labour naturally. I ate a good dinner, not anticipating giving birth in the near future, and at 10 pm I settled down for the night. A bed was made up beside me for Ian, as I hated the idea of him leaving me.

Almost immediately, labour began in earnest. Contractions quickly became strong and regular. Sister took my observations, remarking that the contractions were moderate to strong. I was so relieved, as I had little idea of my own pain threshold and felt that, if these contractions were mild only, I would be needing some strong pain relief before my labour was over.

At 11 pm, I was moved into the labour room and given the mask. I asked for it to be kept at its lowest setting, as I felt the gas did little, but the diversion of breathing into the machine was effective in reducing the pain. The greatest diversion, though, was Ian, talking to me of things, people and places we loved. He spoke again and again of the day before – walking along the beach together, the sea breeze, the smell of the ocean, the salt in the air and the stray dog which accompanied us for much of the time. This provided a very freeing image, one that saturated my consciousness and engaged my senses. With each contraction, I felt I would have to ask for pain relief, then, as it passed, I felt a sense of achievement.

The young midwife assured me that the doctor would arrive in time to deliver the baby, despite it being almost 3 am. In turn, I assured her that I had every confidence in her ability to cope were he not to arrive in time. Ian continued to stand by my side, holding my hand and offering encouragement.

It's a girl!

Just as I felt the overwhelming urge to push, the doctor arrived and, following a few more contractions, the baby's head was delivered. I was helped to sit up, so I could see the baby's head – a slippery ball of blood and vernix and just beautiful. One more push and our baby was born. We had told the midwife earlier we had only one name picked out – nothing for a boy – so, as she was delivered, the midwife did not announce, 'It's a girl', but 'It's Amy!' It was 3 am on Mother's Day.

Ian and I had the baby girl we had hoped for, alive and well. She was three weeks ahead of schedule, though judging by her appearance and lung power she was not at all premature. Amy was immediately checked over by the midwife, then handed to me to be put to the breast. Ian and I were in tears as we held our beautiful bundle. The placenta must have delivered easily, as I was not aware of it coming away. The doctor put a few stitches in my perineum and we were left alone with our child. Ian climbed up on to the messy, narrow, labour-ward delivery table, lay beside me and held me as I cradled Amy in my arms. I could not imagine a happier, more intimate birth anywhere. We had been richly blessed. It was all over... and just beginning.

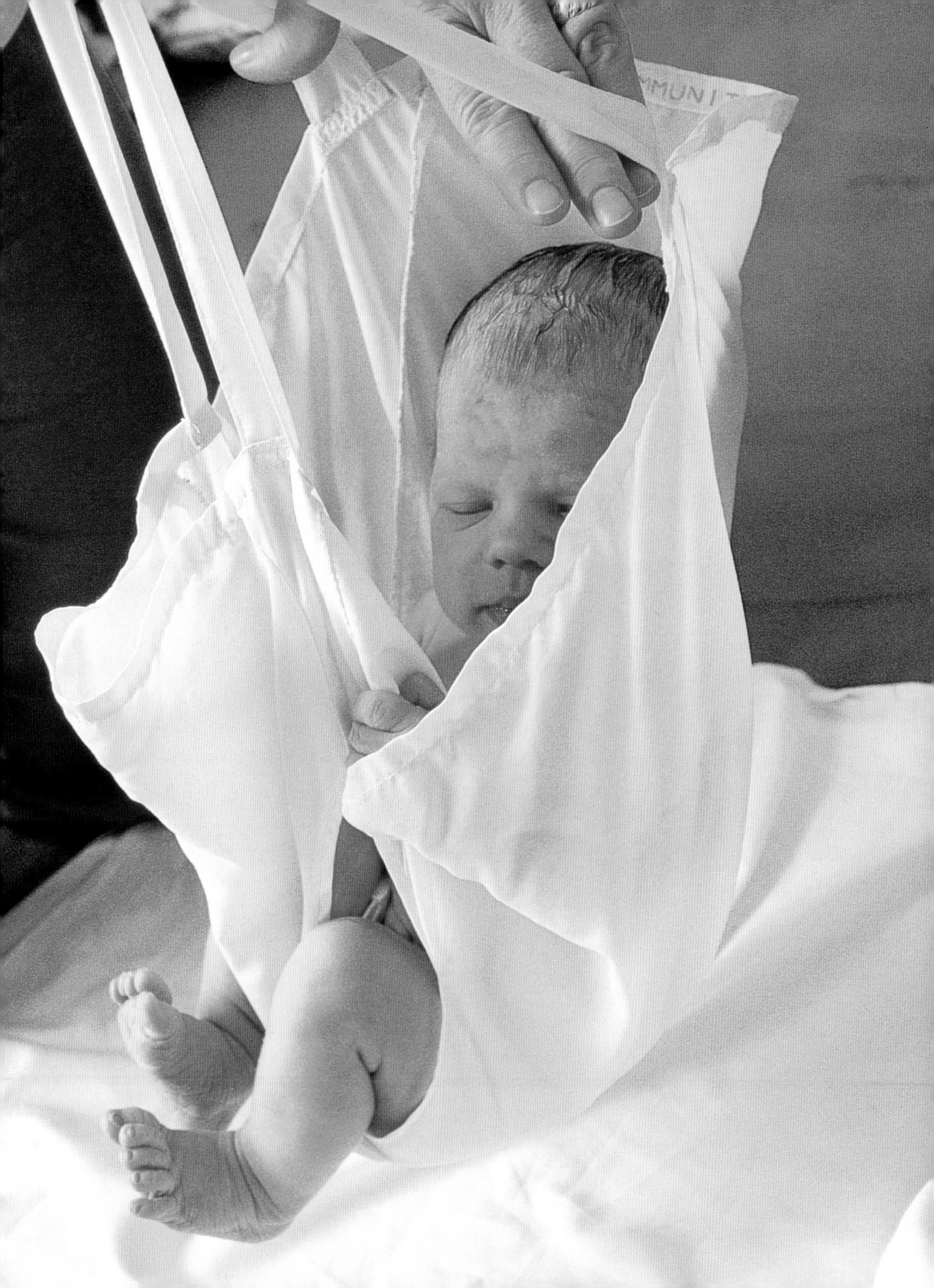

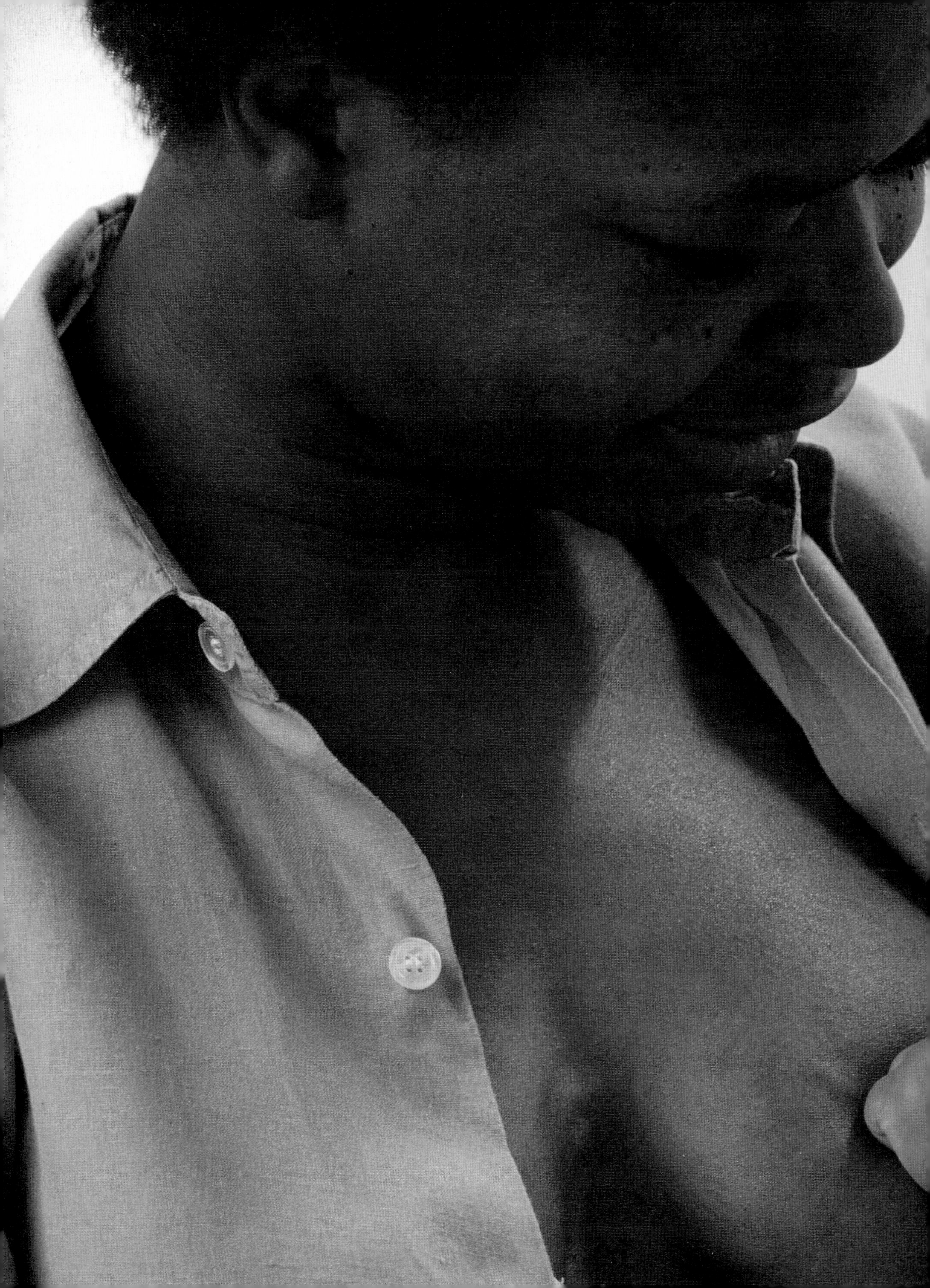

chapter 3

babe in arms

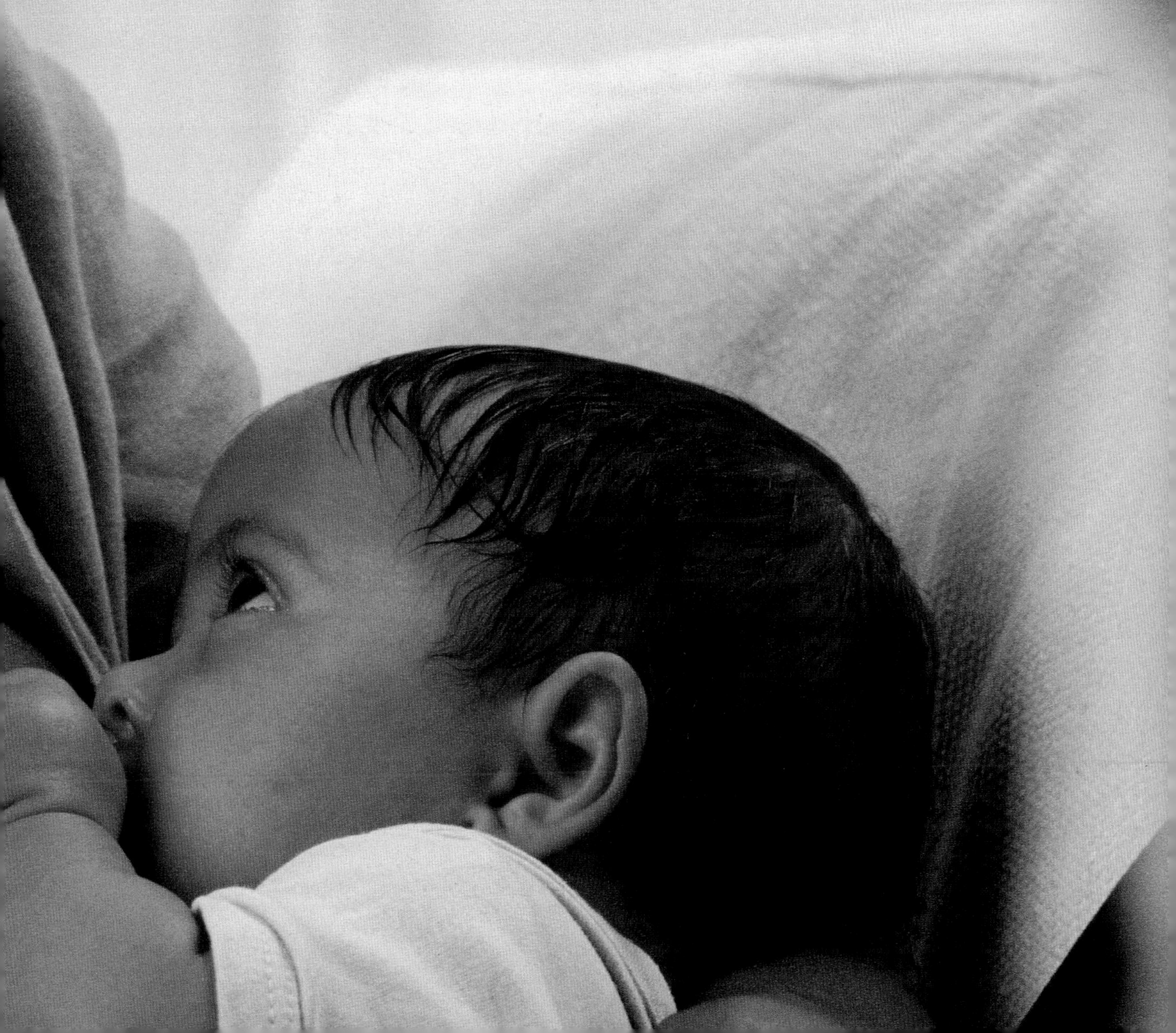

Together at last!

This chapter is about giving babies the love they need, while they are at their most dependent stage – from the moment of birth until they learn to crawl. It's a very important and beautiful time in your life, and a demanding one.

Let's talk about three important aspects to caring for your new baby:

* meeting and bonding with your baby as a separate person
* your growing commitment, expressed through their day-to-day care
* the fun of giving your baby extra learning and stimulation through play.

You are together at last. In the minutes immediately following the excitement of the birth, parents and babies find themselves wrapped in a cocoon of contentment and wellbeing. Most hospitals recognize the importance of letting the new family relax and feel in control. Aside from being able to state their wishes and have resources available to help, parents should be left alone with their baby. A father should be able to sleep in the room, on a stretcher or spare bed, so that he can stay near his partner and help care for the child. Only in the most dire need should the baby be separated from the parents – sleeping in a cot at their bedside, within arm's reach, is usual. This is a wonderful time to start tuning in, a process whereby child and parents can make contact, explore each other and realize, "You are mine and I am yours."

> ***"In the moments following the birth, parents and babies find themselves wrapped in a cocoon of contentment and wellbeing."***

What people do naturally at this time is exactly what's needed. Left alone, parents and baby might gaze into each other's eyes. They might gently explore, look at fingers, legs, shape of mouth, softness of hair, listen to each other's sounds, breathing and murmuring to each other. They might smell, kiss, lick and taste each other.

Bonding through the senses

Bonding – the sense of instantly falling in love with a new baby – is a real thing, and it can feel like magic. But occasionally bonding doesn't just "happen" and new parents can feel disappointed. Medical interventions, or a mother being unconscious or too tired to really be aware at the time of birth, can interrupt the bonding process. We have to actively start building a bond, which will help us to like the baby and find the pleasure in caring for them.

Sight

In the early days and weeks, do lots of gazing with your baby. Sit or lie comfortably together, and simply look into each other's eyes. Research has found the best distance for a baby to focus is about 15 cm (6 in) away (which happens to be the distance to your face when the baby is feeding at the breast). Looking into your baby's eyes, as you soften and relax your gaze, you may notice waves of feelings passing through you. If your child is different to your expectations – not the sex you hoped for, bigger or smaller, or a baby with special needs – this can be an important time to shuttle to and fro in your mind between what you had expected as the form and shape of your baby, and what they are really like. This helps the letting-go process – letting go of "what might have been" and allowing appreciation of "what is".

Sound

Your baby knows your voice and will like to hear it. You will enjoy listening to the baby's breaths and murmurs, and later the babbles and laughter. Babies seem to enjoy the sounds of peaceful music, and your heart beating when they are cuddled against your chest. Babies even like the lilting sounds of talking. Many people sing, and some even read short stories or poems to their babies – reading out aloud has a different rhythm and a sing-song quality. For babies' wellbeing, protect them from harsh, loud and jarring sounds like traffic, loud music and crowds.

Taste

We don't yet understand all that happens when babies and parents kiss and touch. Some subtle chemicals may be exchanged, letting the baby know that "this is Mum" or "this is Dad", and triggering relaxation and trust. Most animals lick their newborns, and babies we have known seem to love having the napes of their necks licked, and their fingers and hands gently sucked – making a game of putting their hands in and out of your mouth, and your little finger in and out of theirs. They will even suck on dad's hairy arms! Kissing must be the softest touch/taste combination that nature could devise. Parents love to kiss and gently move their lips across the

baby's face and hands – even their feet. Babies' first kisses often consist of them opening their mouths wide, falling headlong onto your cheek and licking up and down.

Smells

Babies have an acute capacity to discriminate between smells. They smell your unique combination of skin, hair, sweat and clothing, as well as the smell of mother's milk. They can detect which breast milk comes from their own mother, preferring it to samples taken from other mothers. It is a pleasure for you, too, to smell their skin and hair. In later months, it is valuable to be able to notice smells such as the smell of an ear that is infected or the acid smell of infected urine.

Good things to try

Gentle baby massage

People have been massaging babies for at least 5000 years – probably forever, in fact. It has been proven medically that babies who are touched and stroked lovingly grow faster, recover from illness more quickly, sleep better, have less constipation and fewer digestive problems. They recover from distress more rapidly and are more settled.

Dr Frederic LeBoyer was one of the first people to introduce baby massage to the West. In his book, *Loving Hands*, he recommends that "we have to feed babies, fill them both inside and outside. We must speak to their skins, we must speak to their backs, which thirst and hunger and cry as much as their bellies. Being touched and caressed, being massaged, is food for the infant. Food as necessary as minerals, vitamins and proteins." You don't have to be trained to be able to massage your baby, but it certainly helps to have read about the process and seen photographs of what to do.

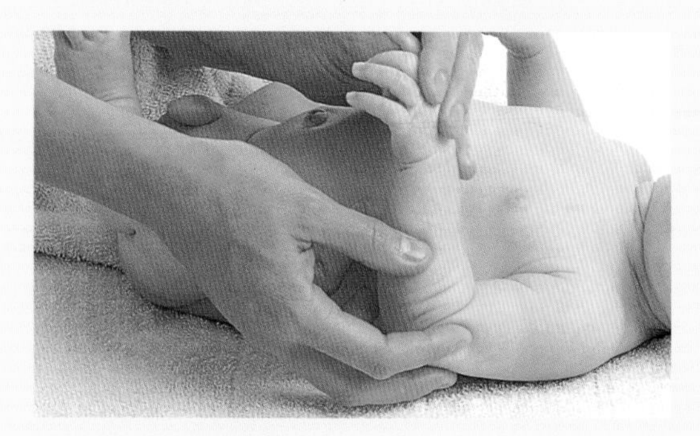

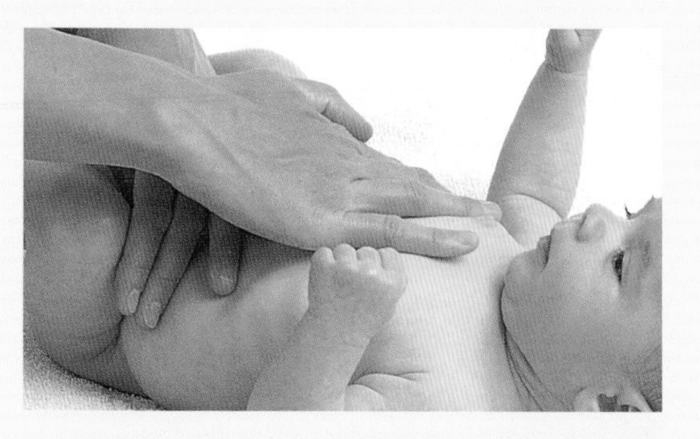

Touch

Although babies can't understand the meaning of the words "I love you", they can feel your loving touch, the comfort and security of being held and the relaxation of being stroked. Specific touches you can enjoy together include massage and special baby yoga. Massage is soothing for you and your baby. Time spent in a warm place stroking the baby's body all over will soothe fretfulness, ease colic, strengthen muscles and promote digestion. You can time it to relax your baby before a feed and a sleep.

Babies need to be held. They are designed to be in someone's arms and this is the most fundamental way that we have to make them feel safe, loved and secure.

Here are some simple guidelines:

- ★ ***enjoy yourself*** – massage in a spirit of calmness and love
- ★ ***don't massage*** straight after a feed
- ★ ***start very gently,*** with light strokes for a short time
- ★ ***take two minutes*** only to massage a newborn infant, working up to a maximum of 10 minutes for a massage with a baby of a few months or older
- ★ ***keep your baby warm*** and make sure you're comfortable. You can sit on the floor with your baby on a towel between your legs; lay your baby on a rug on the floor and kneel above them
- ★ ***take your cues from how the baby is reacting*** – if they are a little fretful, persevere and see if they settle down. If they really don't settle try again another time, when they may be more receptive
- ★ ***babies have very sensitive skin*** – if your baby seems upset by contact with their bare skin, start by stroking their limbs and back with their clothes on, or when they are wrapped in a towel after a bath and you are holding them close
- ★ ***talking and singing*** as you massage all add to the communication and relaxation.

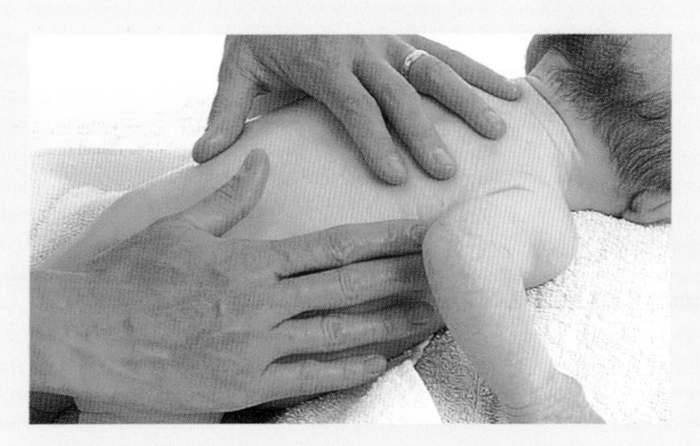

Movement

Inside your womb, your baby has been jiggled when you walk, turned as you roll over in bed, rocked as you move, pressed as you bend, floated in your waters and vigorously massaged by your contractions. The baby's early environment was rich in touch and movement. Once they are outside your body, you naturally want to hold, stroke, snuggle, pat and rock your baby. When someone stands and holds a baby they will almost always start to rock from side to side and sway their hips.

We are very aware of a baby's touch sensations. Without really thinking about it we want to put soft clothes against them, support them in a warm bath for long periods, and ensure they have fresh clean nappies. New parents are often accused of being "too precious" about their newborn. Sometimes people can be quite rough and blasé when handling newborn babies, and it is the new parents who remind us, with their focused concern for their child's wellbeing, that these new babes are indeed precious and in need of empathetic care.

Fathers bond too

Often people think bonding only applies to mothers, but both mothers *and* fathers need to make opportunities for bonding with their baby. U.S. paediatrician and author, Bill Sears, described, in a radio interview, how after several of his own children had been born he started to really get involved in the nurturing of the baby. He believes that fathers need to develop "comforting" skills that are uniquely male. He experimented with holding his baby close, with bare skin-to-skin contact. Also, when he put the baby's ear to his chest, the baby responded well to hearing dad's breathing and heartbeat. His male voice vibrated through the baby's skull when he tucked it up under his neck and held his chin on the top of the baby's head. Lots of fathers we know have found the same things – that they can comfort and entertain, or quieten and put a baby to sleep, by giving their masculine care and attention.

Most fathers will be keen to begin making their own relationship with their new child. They sometimes pick up

their baby and dote on them more than a mother has expected, or even at times more than the mother likes. It's good for the mother to appreciate that this is building a connection that is beneficial for the child and herself in the long term. Dads who care enough to get up in the middle of the night to a crying baby, and who are able to take them for a walk and comfort them well, will be very welcome. At the same time, a father needs to be a little careful to support his partner in connecting with her baby – for instance, if she is groggy from anaesthesia or very tired, he can help her to look at and enjoy the baby as soon as possible. We recommend staying close to home in the first six weeks. Reducing stimulation of people, noise and stress can give you the time you need to relax and get to know each other.

Practical love in action

Bonding isn't just a feeling, it also includes a commitment:

- ★ we have decided we will put ourselves on the line for our child
- ★ we will do the best we can and give our children what they need even if it costs us in time, energy and patience.

Bonding includes what you *do* as well as what you *feel*. Most people will agree that the most important thing a baby needs is love. That's true, but the love we feel towards our baby has to be translated into action. A hundred times a day with a touch of cheek to cheek, gentle handling, soothing caresses, smiles and words, easing their distress with feeding and changing, and by just being there. We put ourselves on call for our baby 24 hours a day. We don't let anyone or anything hurt them. We provide shelter, nourishment and stimulation, even when we would rather watch an exciting moment in a television programme, read a paper, stay asleep or just throw in the towel! That is love. Sometimes it comes easily – at other times it comes right down to a sigh and an effort to push on because the baby needs us. Love is not just the time spent gazing and smiling together like a soap commercial. Every act of assistance is an act of love.

“The single most important thing I have personally learned about motherhood is to keep at it. I've had many different jobs and I've got several qualifications, but with all of these I had the option of ‘chucking it in’. But the job of mothering has been the hardest, because I can't resign or drop out – it's forced me to keep at it through the hard times, and I've learned more self-respect and self-confidence from this than any other thing I've ever done.”

Anne, 38

Getting to know your baby's personality

All babies are unique. It's very clear that they come into the world already equipped with different temperaments. As far back as 1959 it was suggested by researchers that about half of all infants are “easy” (adaptable, happy,

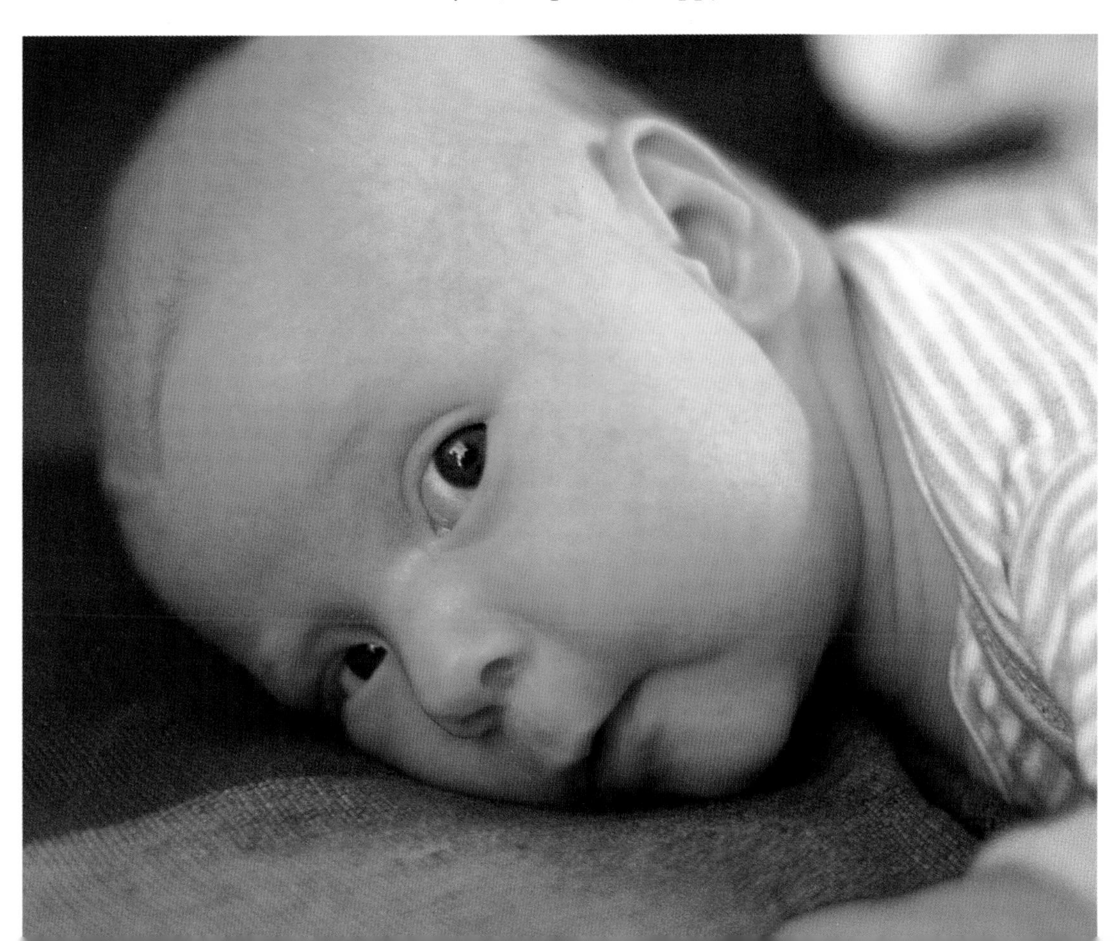

easy to care for); a quarter are easy in routine situations, but have trouble with changes; and another quarter are straight out difficult babies! These have come to be called "High Need Babies" – they can be loud, cranky, overly sensitive to change, with unsettled eating and sleeping habits. These babies can make life pretty tough.

There might be a reason why a baby is difficult – an allergy to cow's milk, say, or an undetected illness – so don't be too quick to label them as "difficult". On the other hand, when all else has been tried, it can be a relief to know that – well – this is just one of those high-need babies.

You and your baby make a unique combination

Below, we have adapted Dr Bill Sears' ideas from his book *The Fussy Baby* to illustrate these different possible combinations. While the diagram is very simplified, it is an easy way to see at a glance what is going on.

The mother-baby combination

You and your baby make a unique combination and the resulting mixture of demands and strengths reflects both your personalities.

You can see "what you are up against", and whether it is you or the baby, or both, that need extra help. Being "high need" or "low need" is of course subject to change, and that's the beauty of it. When a high-need baby tests your strength of character and capacity to endure, the only solution is to become stronger. Not by gritting your teeth, but by calling in all available resources you can from yourself, your partner, family, friends and community support systems. Always remember, the dad can make a big difference to how high- or low-need the mother is, but also be willing to go beyond the family to get the help you need.

Surrendering to your baby's needs

The fashion today is to think that anyone – mother, father, childcare worker, nanny – can interchangeably care for a small baby. Our belief, based on a lot of work with new parents, is that one single adult needs to be the primary carer in the first 12 months of life. This is because such a person adapts themself to the baby's rhythms and needs in such an intense way they function as one unit for the first year. We believe this person should be the mother, unless there are compelling reasons otherwise. The primacy of breastfeeding in the relationship, the way this triggers prolactin release in the bloodstream, which in turn increases mothering feelings, and the tuning out of external distractions, all help to make it easier to have smooth interaction between mother and infant. Studies of the "conversation" between mothers and very young babies reveal an intricate and synchronized pattern of responses which seem to teach the baby and the mother to read each other's signals and be harmonized and secure. Babies thrive on familiarity.

A father in this situation has a different role – part of his contribution to the child comes through supporting and facilitating the mother-child bond. This doesn't mean he doesn't have his own relationship with the child, but that he is willing to take second place, knowing the child will move towards him more in time because of the security they feel with their mother. It's a matter of sequencing, knowing that balance comes over time and needn't be forced artificially to happen all at once. The issue of roles is a delicate one, because it can be misinterpreted. It can be taken to mean

'The Long Night'

She is sick, the small mound of her stomach is like a hot plate. Her legs are no cooler. I know I need to lower her temperature but if I attempt to ease the eiderdown off her body, she scolds me and pulls it back. She has a heavy cold which, unbeknown to us, has flared into an ear infection. Her mother has been dispatched to another bed in the vain hope that she might find sleep there. The child and I will spend the night together — grabbing at insubstantial clouds of sleep, waking to her pain, making stumbling forays to the bathroom in search of the medicine. Her comfort is to play with other people's ear lobes. We have lain there for some hours, marooned in bleak sleeplessness, when I gently try to disengage from her. I ask her not to hold my ears; it keeps me awake and I am trying to go to sleep. It had not occurred to me that she would be trying to make the best of her ordeal, to be brave. "I trying to sleep too," she retorts, and suddenly her hot little face is wet and shuddering, and her avalanche of tears is a measure of what she has endured. The platform we stand on as parents — all-knowingness — has opened like a hangman's trap-door beneath me. In its place is a red mist which feels uncomfortably like shame, but there is also a knowledge that I have never loved this child more deeply and that I shall never forget this night.

that mothers must stay home and raise the children, while fathers trudge off to work and feel excluded, and this is not our meaning. What we are saying is that in the first year or two, life works better if a baby is the number one priority for one adult, and that the mother has certain advantages for this job. This might not always be the case, and other arrangements might work too. Be sensitive to what is right for your family.

What young parents urgently need is more flexibility in work hours, parental leave, and financial support for young families, and extra help in the home so that couples can find their own balance.

Finding harmony

From the very start, you and your new baby will be working towards a harmony. It's like a dance where you gradually learn the steps together. You smile and they smile. They cry and you pick them up. You rock them and they fall gently asleep. They become trusting and settled and you become more confident.

Something you try may work one time and not another, so you move on and try something else. You gradually increase your "repertoire". For example, what can you do for crying babies? Here are some of the possibilities:

- ★ feed them
- ★ change them
- ★ pat them
- ★ rock them
- ★ sing to them
- ★ put them to bed
- ★ give them a dummy
- ★ make them warmer
- ★ burp them
- ★ hold them
- ★ stroke their back
- ★ talk to them soothingly
- ★ take them for a walk
- ★ play music
- ★ put them in a bouncer
- ★ push them in the pram
- ★ make them cooler
- ★ smile and talk to them
- ★ let them sit up and watch the family
- ★ ask for help from family or friends
- ★ position them to relax their cramped stomach muscles (draped across your lap, face down)
- ★ seek help from an osteopath
- ★ ring a support group (see p. 232), or another parent helpline
- ★ seek medical advice.

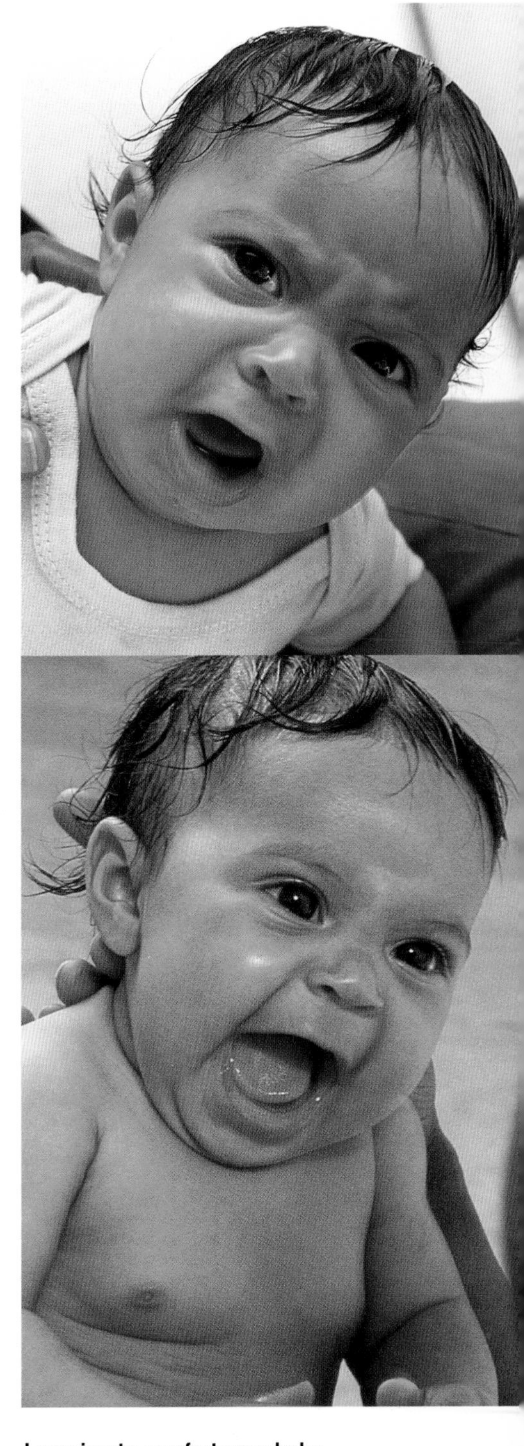

Learning to comfort your baby and fulfil their needs will usually change their tears to smiles

Which of these methods you try will depend on what you know of your child, and the situation. You ask yourself – are they likely to be tired, or have they just woken up and had a feed. Does your baby's face look 'pained' or is it a slowing down, sleepy cry?

> *Our baby was diagnosed as having colic, which just gave it a name – no solution! The impression our doctor gave us was that we just had to put up with it. We hated hearing our baby cry in so much pain, and thinking that there might be months of this distress. We found a paediatrician who gave us good, helpful, practical advice. We learned not to give up too easily.*
>
> **Patrick, 27**

The best kind of help you can get from other parents and professionals is not bossy prescriptions, but rather the sharing of ideas to help you increase your repertoire of new things to try with your baby. Because each child is so different no one thing works all the time. Babies teach us to be flexible. We learn to persist. A crying baby won't stop just because you close the door, or are tired and need a break, or the phone is ringing, or you want desperately to go to the toilet! The baby's nature is to insist and your job is to persist. Watch them for their responses, learn what they like and provide it, then pat yourself on the back.

It usually takes only a few weeks to really start to understand a baby's particular patterns. We help them:

- ★ to feel comfortable – with a bath or massage, change of nappy and clothes
- ★ to tire themselves out – by letting them kick about and exercise
- ★ to feel satisfied – by feeding them
- ★ to feel secure and lulled into sleep – by cuddles, warmth and gentleness.

We try to time all of these activities so that they are completed by the end of the day. During the night, we try to help the baby – feed or change or comfort them without bright lights, noise or chatter, talking quietly, singing a gentle song. Sitting quietly rocking or stroking them, but not stimulating them so much that they become wide awake. Before long, the baby begins to sleep longer at nights so we can sleep too. By doing the same things the same way, the baby settles into a routine rhythm. At least, that's the idea.

Patterns help everyone

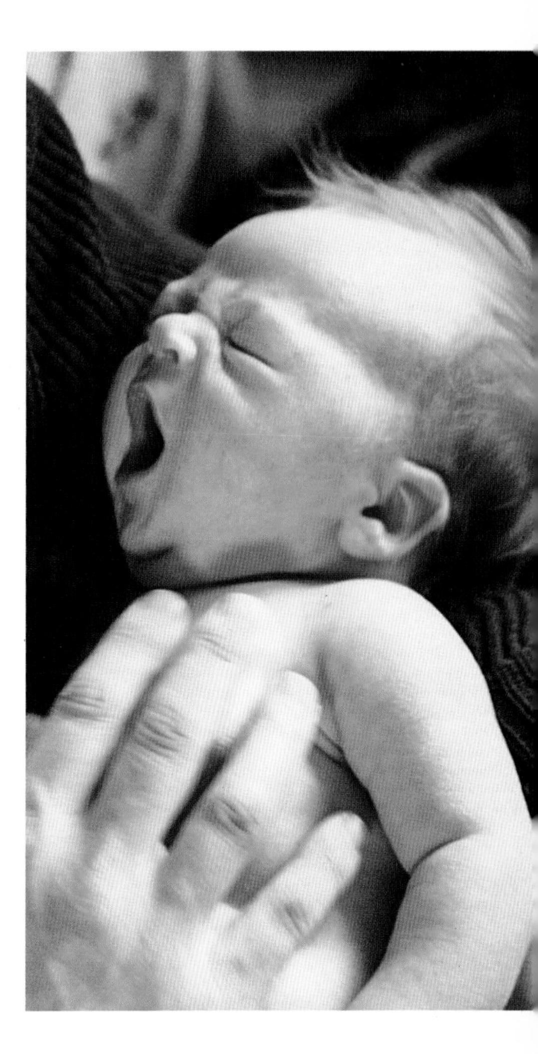

We all like to feel some sense of order or constancy in our lives. Part of the constancy lies in the patterns – the rhythm of things that organize our time so everything fits in and has a place. The rhythm of the seasons, night and day, and rest and activity, are important stabilizing and rejuvenating forces in human life, the in-breath and out-breath of our lives.

Babies have their own rhythms and cycles too, which naturally grow into more adult-friendly timing as they get older. Artificially imposing routines on babies – such as strict four-hourly feeds – was a clumsy and often damaging way to make babies fit the adult world long before they were ready to do so.

Thankfully we have become much more natural in our parenting today. Being natural doesn't mean being chaotic, though. There is a natural kind of routine which both babies and parents benefit from, and this is arrived at gradually.

Life with a newborn baby seems very chaotic to begin with, since they are not concerned with day or night – only hunger, rest and wakefulness. They have been in the dark for nine months and are not too concerned about what time of day it is.

The best approach seems to lie in the parents adapting to the baby at first (for example, snatching rests while baby naps). Gradually the baby's cycle extends and settles down into longer phases of waking and sleeping. Parents help the baby most by being sensitive and available, so the baby learns to trust that their needs will always be met, and their bodies adapt to accept longer spells of alertness and exercise, and more nutrition. Because the baby is not jarred into an adult pattern, but rather coaxed, they are able to settle into a pattern that works for everyone.

Every family has its own creative methods of tackling the "big sleep problem". Here are some parents stories about how they helped their babies and toddlers with sleeping...

Parents' stories

How they helped their babies to sleep

"Little Mattie used to like to be rocked to sleep – I ended up buying an old rocking chair and it stopped my back from aching and I found it very soothing too."

"We found it helped to lay Tilda on her side in the bed and slowly pat her back or bottom – the timing was like a heartbeat, a slow and steady rhythm till she fell asleep."

"When Mara was very little, she would startle as she was falling asleep, and wake up all over again. We found she was much more secure with a blanket wrapped around her, holding her up to the chest and singing softly to her. When she fell asleep we would put her on her back and unwrap the blanket loosely so she could move her arms in her sleep. It even seemed to help to place her with her feet against the foot end of the cot so she could feel something solid. She would startle if she found herself with nothing secure around her."

"Gradually we seemed to find a pattern that helped Sven to get off to sleep. We would change him, read his little cardboard book to him, pull the curtains shut, give him his teddy and cover him with his soft blanket. Then we would give him a kiss goodnight, and quietly leave him. Mission accomplished."

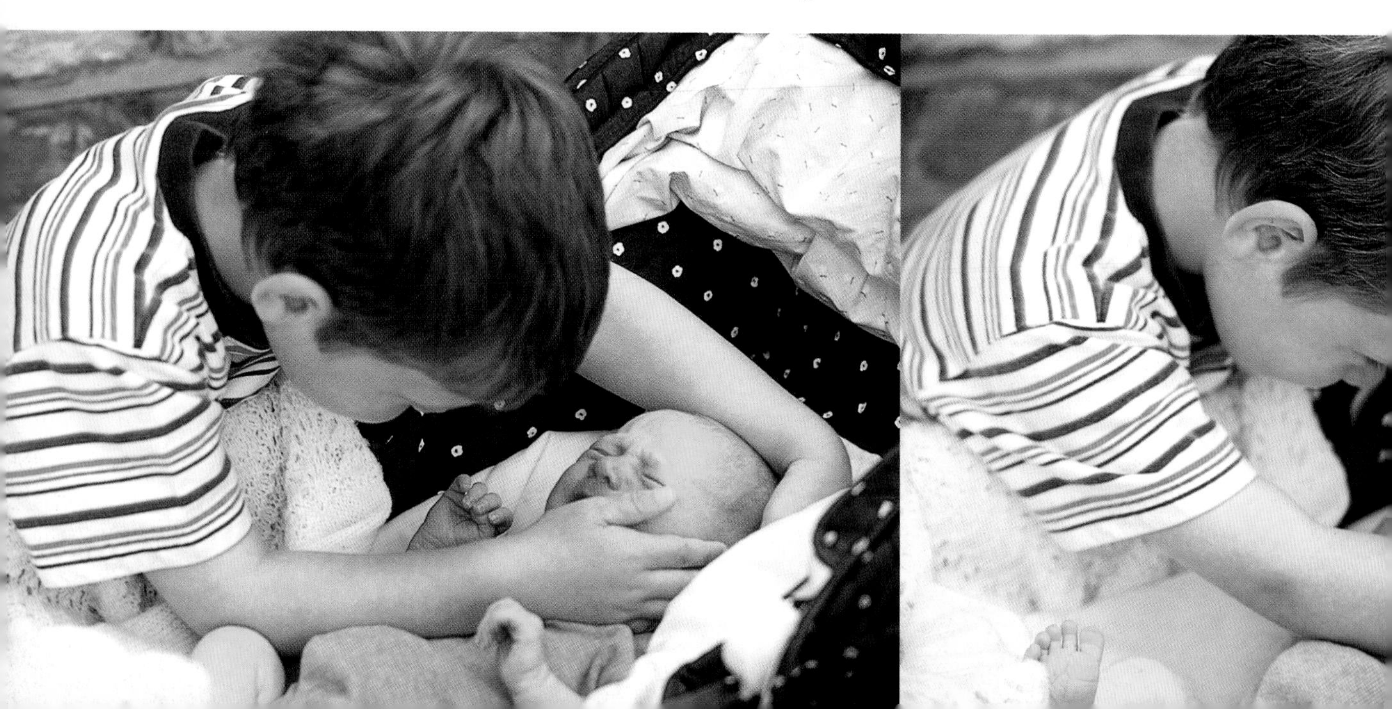

The mobile baby who wakes at night

"At first I didn't mind the night feeds but over time they were increasing, not decreasing as they were supposed to. My clinic sister sugggested that maybe Donna needed more solid foods in the daytime, and she assured me that babies over six months don't need night feeds and I should decide for myself if it was a problem or not."

"We always slept with Zoe in our bed. She had the spot where the mattress meets the wall. We loved her being so close, and it was so easy and natural to turn over to feed her and go back to sleep again. But after about nine months, I felt we were all disturbing each other. The way we went about it was to get her a cot next to the bed. Then later when she was about two, a mattress on the floor. We moved the mattress gradually closer to the door, and then we got her to sleep on the mattress in her sister's room in the daytime. Then she got a special new bed for her birthday, and has slept in it in the room she shares with her sister ever since."

"Daylight saving time, when the clocks are turned back an hour, really messed up our routines! Then we realized that it was the early light in Tom's room that was waking him, so we just got thicker curtains."

There is a deeper point to be made here – that as adults our lives have become terribly removed from the health-giving cycles of the seasons, natural light and the chance

to really rest and heal. Mobile phones disturb us on weekends, we work late into the night, grab snacks instead of sitting down for meals, and so on. Yet until we find a calm rhythm of our own, we cannot provide this for our children. Just as we breathe in and breathe out we can alternate rest and activity in a healthy rhythm. By doing this, we find that we can stay energized much more of the time.

A method for getting used to have-to's

"We have to help our babies to enjoy the things that are unavoidable, or at least do them painlessly."

There are some things that babies just have to do which they don't always take to kindly. They might hate being bathed, changed or strapped into their car safety seat. Sadly in the modern world we can't just let babies wander naked in the garden, or take them everywhere on foot. We have to help them to enjoy the things that are unavoidable, or at least do them painlessly. There are three steps to teaching a baby to get used to something:

1 *start slowly*
2 *make it enjoyable*
3 *persist.*

Here are some parents tips on how to do this in three typical activities:

The bath

(start slowly)

"I had to undress her while holding her very close to me. Either on my lap or against my chest, or with my face very near her as she lay on her back. I slowly took off her clothes. Then I would let her look at the water for a while and watch me run my fingers through it. Then I would gently let her foot touch it and warm her toes – all very gradually while holding her, even when she was sitting in the water. I threaded my arm around her back and held her arm."

Make routine tasks an enjoyable activity for both of you.

(make it enjoyable)
"I used to take him in the bath with me. If he lay on top of my chest I could lower myself to increasingly drop deeper into the water, till his lower body was covered by the water. His great payoff was enjoying a breastfeed while having his bath. It wasn't long before he enjoyed bathing on his own."

(persist)
"We could only get him to sit happily in the water for a minute or two and then we would get him out as soon as he cried, hug him in a dry towel, then put him back in the water again. His confidence increased because he knew we'd get him out whenever he cried. He gradually stayed longer as he got more used to it."

Changing nappies

(start slowly)

"I try not to rush it. Luckily when they are very young, they are more interested in looking at you and don't seem to notice. I just make sure the room is warm and they don't feel suddenly all naked and exposed. I try not to pull faces or make yuk sounds when the nappy comes off! "

(make it enjoyable)

"I let her enjoy kicking her legs freely, after I've cleaned her up. We chatter and I tickle her and say little rhymes to her. It's a lovely close time."

(persist)
"As my babies got a little older, I made the nappy changes quicker and more brisk if they seemed impatient. I changed them on a mat on the floor as it was less dangerous, as they were now more able to roll or throw themselves about."

"I think they got a bit sick of it as they got older, but that was a good thing, as they and I were both ready to put the nappies away for good, and they were more motivated to use the potty!"

Car seats

(start slowly)
"We would have to pick the best time to travel. Sometimes it was when he was ready to sleep. Sometimes straight after a bottle and a change. Then we would only make short journeys at first, or if it was a longer journey we would make frequent stops and get him out, and cuddle him, then go on."

(make it enjoyable)
"We found someone needed to sit in the back with her and pat her or hold her hand and talk to her as we drove along. We tied a few small toys to her seat so she could haul them up and play with them as we went along. As she got older we used music tapes that she only had in the car, and she could eat a small snack or have a bottle as we travelled."

(persist)
"It took about a year I would say, then our son started to be able to get excited about where we were going and who we would see. As soon as he saw the keys and I said his sister's name, he would run to the door ready to go and pick her up from school."

Reducing the risk of cot death

Research is helping us learn to prevent cot death. Since 1991, the rate of cot death has been halved by parents following the five guidelines on the right.

When to go straight to the doctor

Health authority advice is that there may be serious illness if your baby has any of the following symptoms:

- **has a high-pitched or weak cry,** is less responsive, is much less active or more floppy than usual
- **looks very pale** all over, grunts with each breath, has obvious dips in the upper tummy or between the ribs as he or she breaths
- **takes less than a third** of usual fluids, passes much less urine than usual, vomits green fluid, or passes blood in motions
- **has a high fever with sweating**
- **if your baby seems unwell** seek medical advice early and quickly.

Urgent medical attention is needed if your baby:

- **stops breathing or goes blue**
- **is unresponsive** and shows no awareness of what is going on
- **has glazed eyes** and does not focus on anything
- **cannot be woken**
- **has a fit.**

5 things to remember

1 Place your baby on their back to sleep

The risk of cot death is reduced if babies are not put on their tummy to sleep. Place your baby on their back to sleep. Side sleeping is not as safe as sleeping on the back, but is much safer than sleeping on the front. Older babies can turn over and move around the cot. Put them on their back, but let them find their own sleeping position. The risk of cot death in babies over six months is extremely low.

2 Don't let your baby get too hot (or too cold)

Overheating can increase the risk of cot death. Babies can overheat because of too much bedding or clothing, or because the room is too hot.

When you check your baby, if he or she is sweating or the tummy feels hot to touch, take off some of the bedding. Don't worry if your baby's hands or feet feel cool, this is normal.

Babies do not need hot rooms, all-night heating is rarely necessary. Keep the room at a temperature that is comfortable to you. About 18°C (65°F) is comfortable. In summer, if it is very warm, the baby may not need any bedclothes other than a sheet.

Even in winter, most babies who are unwell or feverish need fewer clothes. Babies lose excess heat from their heads, so make sure the head cannot be covered with bedclothes. Babies should never sleep with a hot-water bottle or electric blanket, next to a radiator, heater or fire, or in direct sunshine. Duvets or quilts, baby nests, sheepskins, wedges, bedding rolls, cot bumpers and pillows may carry a risk of overheating. Remove hats and extra clothing as soon as you come indoors or enter a warm car, bus or train, even if it means waking your baby.

3 Keep your baby's head uncovered in their cot

Place your baby in the "feet-to-foot" position. Babies whose heads are covered accidentally with bedding are at an increased risk of cot death. To prevent your baby wriggling down under the covers place your baby's feet at the foot of the cot and make the bed up so that the covers reach no higher than the shoulders. Covers should be securely tucked in so they cannot slip over the baby's head. If your baby is unwell, seek advice promptly. Babies often have minor illnesses which you do not need to worry about. Make sure your baby drinks plenty of fluids and is not too hot. If your baby sleeps a lot, wake him or her regularly for a drink. The column on the far left tells you when you should go to the doctor.

4 Sleep in the same room as your baby

Babies who slept in the same room as their parents for the first six months of their life had a significantly reduced risk.

5 Smoking is a risk

Smoking in pregnancy increases the risk of cot death. It is best not to smoke at all, but the less you smoke, the lower the risk. Don't let anyone smoke in the same room as your baby. It is best if nobody smokes in the house, including visitors. Do not take your baby into smoky places. If you smoke, sharing a bed with your baby may increase the risk of cot death.

- Remember that cot death is rare, so please don't let worry about cot death stop you enjoying your baby's first few months.
- FSID recommends that all parents learn how to resuscitate a baby. For information on resuscitation training courses, contact St John Ambulance www.St-john-ambulance.org.uk/, your local Red Cross or ask at your local hospital.

Source: *Foundation for the Study of Infant Death Website:* http://www.sids.org.uk/fsid
Always look for up-to-date advice by consulting the website or asking your doctor. New research is happening all the time.

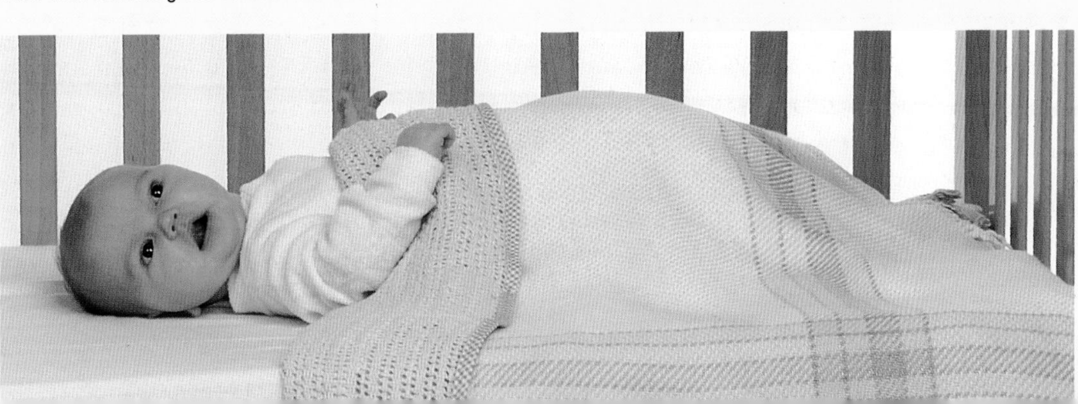

Feet-to-foot means laying the baby on their back with their feet touching the foot of the cot.

Looking after yourself

New mothers can feel quite "fragile" for some time after the baby's birth, although many are pleasantly surprised by their rapid recovery. A new mother is entitled to take time out to rest and enjoy her baby, and other people need to pamper her, respect her and help her to do this.

This is a time when you shouldn't have to move mountains or prove how spectacularly you can perform. If parents can be physically and emotionally supported for the first few weeks, when demands are high and many adjustments are taking place, they will find they have more to give their new child and each other. It will then be easier for them to care for their baby, and things are more likely to go well. If you care about babies, care for their mothers and support their fathers.

"I distinctly remember the sheer pleasure and relief when a nurse brought me a hot chocolate drink and a biscuit at about 5 am one morning. I was sitting feeling lonely, sore and lost, with nothing to do but wait for the baby to wake up. I felt like someone had snuggled me up and made me feel cared for. I needed for myself what my baby needed from me."

Stephanie, 40

Helping hands

A friend of ours has this wonderful saying – "Visitors Are Fair Game". Anyone who is lovingly involved enough to want to visit the new baby and parents, or who has the temerity to visit at such a special time, can be pressed into service. They can be asked to wash up, vacuum, make a bed, chop vegetables, prepare cups of tea and snacks, turn on the washing machine and hang out clothes, hold the

baby, go to the shops, or anything else your creativity conjures up. We know of a family who had twins and were in real trouble handling the workload. A friend circulated a list asking other friends to put their names down to give either cash, food or time! If you are shy, put up a big list in clear view of the front door. Entitle it "Ways you can help". Your friends will feel pleased at being able to help out in a practical way.

During a recent high-stress time for our family, a friend of ours began preparing and delivering an evening meal to our house about once a week! She also picked up the crockery next day without even stopping to make conversation. It was a priceless contribution to our wellbeing, definitely the last casserole that saved the camel's back!

“ *When my mother was having her babies, it was the accepted thing that the new mother could get outside help – a paid helper to clean and cook for about six weeks after the birth. This wasn't just for rich people, everyone did it. There was no stigma attached. In other words, you weren't suspected of that dreaded disease "not coping". It was just accepted as necessary.* ”

Julie, 36

Importance of rest

Learn to get your rest in short breaks when the baby is asleep. Put your feet up, have a drink and consciously let go of your muscles, close your eyes, breathe easily and deeply. Use the time when you are feeding the baby to rest as well. In short, rest when the baby rests. If you've had a restful kind of pregnancy, daytime naps will come easily. If you've been busy and rushed during the pregnancy, it may take some deliberate determination to retrain yourself.

It's a trap to use the baby's rest time to rush about tidying. A "good" mother is a slob for these few months. Your wellbeing and that of the baby is more important than the housework. Your body knows what it wants and, when allowed to, will often fall asleep when the baby goes down and wake, two hours later, when baby does, thinking "what happened?". If you know or can learn meditation, you'll find this very effective too. Ten minutes

Good things to try

Beautiful baby

This is great for when you're feeling low and maybe not enjoying your baby much. Perhaps your baby is teething or has a cold and is wakeful with the snuffles. This is a good way to cheer you both up. Dress up your baby in special clothes, choosing the ones you most like to see them in. Apart from being warm and convenient, children's clothes are made to please the eye of mothers and other admirers. Another way to feel better is to remind yourself of the good, funny times by looking at photographs of your baby.

★ ***Gazing at your baby*** in their "Sunday Best" may help you to like them again. Dressing up your baby at home for yourself or before visiting town, the child-health clinic, or relatives or friends. Total strangers will say, "What a beautiful baby!" and you will glow with pride as you head down the street. Grandparents and other relatives will be adoring fans, too, and all this can magnify your enthusiasm for parenting.

★ ***Take lots of photographs*** and share them with family and friends. It's nearly always worth ordering two sets of prints, as relatives love to have photos of children, especially if they live at a distance. There are reasons other than generosity for giving photos away. A family we know had a house fire which destroyed all their photos and records. But, to their delight, people were able to send back copies of photos they thought they would never see again.

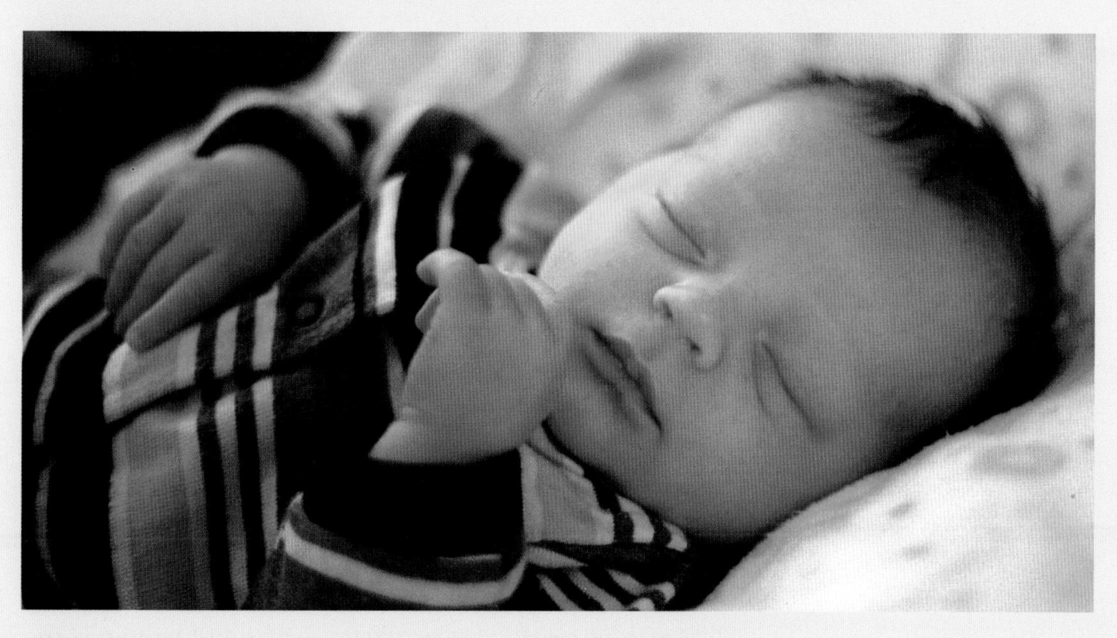

of meditation can be worth an hour or more of sleep. Listening to music or relaxation tapes is another way to relax more deeply.

Giving yourself a chance to relax is also a way to have a calmer, more settled baby, because a baby will always respond to your level of serenity. Even if you are both awake, a restless baby can be calmed by you or your partner lying with them and listening quietly to beautiful music.

Sharing the load

From the beginning, you and your partner need to work out who does what. You can vary this to suit, but if the load is shared, it becomes possible to carry.

“*The way we got through those bad months, with a sick baby, cold weather and a terrible house, was to help each other continually. My husband would sleep in another room, and get a good night's sleep. Baby Susan would wake up and have a feed perhaps six times a night. I could comfort her back to sleep by having her in my arms. When she awoke fully at about 6 am, I would be exhausted from light and broken sleep, and my husband would come in and get her and change her, play with her and give her breakfast while I slept. He'd also supervise the other kids getting fed and ready for the day. Just when he was ready to leave for work, he'd wake me and I'd take over again. By then the baby would be ready for a mid-morning nap, so I could clean up the house, have a shower, and eat some breakfast in peace!*”

Sally Anne, 29

> *When my husband, Rob, gets home from work, there is a time he takes with our son, Jackson, that I really enjoy. He plays with Jackson and they have a bath together. I can get tea and still have a bit of time to myself. We eat, then Jackson goes off to sleep, and Rob and I have a couple of hours to be together and unwind.*
>
> **Wendy, 35**

We once asked husbands in a couples' communication group for their advice on how to help. Their suggestions were:

- ★ bring home take-away food
- ★ do the ironing – become an Iron Man!
- ★ clean up the house when mother and baby collapse in sleep

* pick up as you go along, tidy as you walk and never add to mess in the kitchen or living room
* guard against unwanted visitors and diplomatically fend off intrusions
* do a late-night laundry shift
* organize family members as babysitters
* play with or take out older children
* buy an answerphone and choose who to speak to.

Finally, an older man regaled the group with this story:

"We were older parents, and had always said that a baby would just have to fit into our routines, that there was no need for disruption in our lives. We wouldn't let our lives revolve around a baby like these younger couples seemed to do. Ha! The reality was different. The baby would just never sleep at night, and had colic the whole time, and would scream with discomfort after a feed. The only thing that calmed him down was to walk with him over my shoulder for hours on end. When I stopped walking he started screaming again. If I put him down he woke up! I just want everyone to know that walking around the inner suburbs at 3 am with a bundle slung over my shoulder is what I want to be doing. This baby has not changed my life!" (Much laughter from the group.)

Recharge your own battery

A group of mothers at a child-health clinic brainstormed a list of things to do during the day to boost your energy and pick yourself up.

They included:

* have a cup of tea
* ring and chat to a friend
* go to Grandma's house with the children
* take the baby for a walk in the pram
* sit outside in the sun
* read a magazine
* eat chocolate
* play tennis while the baby is minded, or let him watch from his pram
* watch a favourite soap

New mothers can feel fragile and overwhelmed – as vulnerable as their new baby.

★ take a shower
★ bathe with the baby
★ meditate
★ exercise
★ brush your hair, put on make up and make yourself look good
★ go to a local shop, take your time and chat to the owners
★ invite friends over with their babies, for adult company
★ eat snacks or have a nourishing drink
★ do craft work.

Occasionally, on really hard days, if you have been unwell or pressured, decide to have a time-out day. For many of us, it's not possible to have a reliable and loving helper to take the baby off our hands, so we have to do the best we can to have an easy day and allow our batteries to recharge. Don't do anything that isn't essential. Forget housework and extra jobs; your aim is to relax as deeply as possible and to enjoy your baby.

New mother – old feelings

Sometimes it seems that old feelings from your past can surface in the present. Often a mother with a new baby starts to feel as if she is an infant herself – fragile, overwhelmed, frightened, unable to think clearly, emotionally distressed and vulnerable. This may be because she is re-experiencing the time of her own birth. But if a new mother is treated with tenderness and nurturing, she will gradually find her strength and self-assurance returning.

A new mother's partner and other carers can help tremendously by gently encouraging her to think through her options. They also have an important role in protecting her from too many intrusions, and the need to make a lot of decisions. Helpers are of great value too, if they nurture her with food, encouragement, massage, bed-making, house-cleaning, washing and ironing, keeping her warm, and comforting and caring for the baby. This can be done with respect and thoughtfulness, not by taking over and ordering her off to bed.

In the rare instances where a woman has severe depression – where desperate thoughts occur to her often, and family or friends fear for her safety or that of the baby – then professional help should be sought immediately.

Usually, it is the simple and practical little things which are of the most help to a new mother. The point is, it takes time and learning to get it right with your baby, especially as their needs are constantly changing and unfolding. You show your love actively, and show your commitment by experimenting to find what makes your baby happy. Soon you will be operating smoothly and with ever greater confidence.

Awakening the Tigress Mother

All mothers have inside them a "being" or part of their character that they might not have known existed, yet which is essential for the job of mothering. In some mothers it is instantly and obviously there the moment their child is born, in other people it needs some help to awaken. This part is ancient, powerful and fiercely protective of young life. It has many names around the world, but we call it the Tigress Mother.

To help you contact this part of yourself, we suggest you experience what it might be like, from the child's point of view, to be the recipient of Tigress protection. Can you recall ever having been completely safe? Can you imagine what it would be like to rest in the total security of a large and powerful caregiver? Someone who is totally protective, and is dedicated to caring for and respecting you and your needs?

Imagine a truly competent and deeply warm human being who for a while can take care of everything to do with the outside world. They have your wellbeing and best interests totally at heart. Can you feel a sense of relaxation and relief at the pleasure of just being, without having to do anything?

In everyday life we may have small glimpses of this degree of safety – with a competent and generous partner; from caring family members and wise and helpful friends. Some of us may have little of this experience, and feel that in life we have to battle on alone. But secure, trusting and relaxed is what the child in the Tigress's care can feel.

Now, at this point, think of a tigress, large and powerful, standing guard over her cubs, and imagine that you are this tiger mother. Does it surprise you how easily you can imagine the teeth, claws and powerful muscles of a tigress? This is a fierce strength. You will find you can call on this strength, for alertness and endurance, or when incredible effort is required, many times during the growing years of your children. As you think of your baby, you'll realize that you have made a commitment to

this little person to protect and provide for them because they are totally helpless without you. This may come easily, or it may be very tough, depending on you and your circumstances. Nonetheless, the bottom line is, a baby must be looked after – by you or by someone else you have chosen for their competence and care. The tigress in you keeps you going until things improve.

Awakening the Tigress is one of the many beneficial effects of becoming a mother. It doesn't make you invincible, but it provides energy, commitment and intuition which you may never have known you had. The Tigress may develop gradually, or might suddenly be there in a crisis. The result is the same. You realize quite simply that you would protect this child with your life. It's the energy to do the very best that you possibly can. Denise's story perfectly illustrates the force of the awakened Tigress.

"*Awakening the Tigress... provides energy, commitment and intuition which you may never have known you had...It's the energy to do the very best that you possibly can.*"

"*When I was expecting my second son, I had a strong intuition that something was wrong with this baby. In my mind I thought it might be some deformity, perhaps a club foot; and I guess in my mind I was trying to focus on something simple and understandable. So I was very alert at the birth, and totally keyed up to that moment when I would know if there was anything wrong. It was in the days when you lay on your back with your legs in stirrups, and when the baby came out there was a peculiar hush in the room. I asked, "What is it? What's wrong?" The doctor looked over at me with a kindly look and said, "It's a boy, and he's got a cleft palate, but we'll take care of him for you." They proceeded to bundle him up in a warm blanket. At this point I did something which seems physically impossible looking back – I sat right up, even with my legs still in the stirrups, and yelled, "Give him to me!" which they did! I still see that doctor from time to time around town, and he has always treated me with respect and perhaps a touch of awe.*

My son needed a lot of surgery and assistance and went through many operations until he was 16 years old. After that last operation, I went to bed and stayed there and cried for days and days. People were concerned about me, but I knew exactly what was happening – I was letting go of the 16 years of effort to get him back where he needed to be. I could now let myself be tired, vulnerable, and I could grieve, but up until then this Tigress energy had sustained me. ❞

Denise, 47

Breastfeeding

Comedian Robin Williams describes how, after six months of pregnancy, the most wondrous thing happens – the Breast Fairy comes! Both men and women are surprised, curious and delighted by the rounding and ripening of the mother-to-be's breasts and nipples as pregnancy proceeds. However, these changes are mild compared to the changes after the birth, when breasts seem to take on a life of their own!

A few days after your baby is born, you wake up to find two little rock hard mountains where your soft comfy breasts used to be! The milk has "come in". In the few days prior to this, your baby will have been practising sucking and getting small amounts of the incredibly nutritious, golden colostrum. Your baby has been building an appetite, and thank goodness for that, because you very quickly discover you need each other! Often a new mother finds herself watching her sleeping newborn and hoping madly that the baby will wake up soon and help relieve her of her abundant milk supply. This supply-and-demand link-up primes you to stay close and have frequent and regular contact through the breastfeeds.

Pleasure and pain

Women have varying reactions to breastfeeding. Some find enormous pleasure in the whole process, and are sad when the time comes to wean their toddlers off the breast. Some are happy to do it, but pleased to stop. Others are unable to breastfeed because of difficulties, while others just prefer to give the whole thing a miss and feed with a bottle of formula. Many factors affect whether you start to breastfeed, and how long you continue. You will be trying for a balance between what your head and heart dictate.

The sensations that accompany breastfeeding are surprisingly strong at first. The "letdown" reflex is a feeling triggered just after the baby has begun to suck. There is a "release" feeling in both breasts simultaneously. The nipples become erect, and both breasts fill with milk from the storage ducts deeper in your chest and underarms. Sometimes in the early days, your baby's suckling will stimulate cramping feelings in your uterus, called "afterpains". These are caused by the uterus contracting back to its pre-pregnancy size.

Mastering the art

While your baby is busy on one side, the other breast may squirt milk out, so you'll need a pad to catch the overflow. You'll come to know the slightly metallic smell of breastmilk, waking and sleeping! You'll get used to being damp, changing shirts a lot and going around padded up like a teenager with socks in her bra! In time, you'll learn to take this with good humour. What else can you do when you discover you've been out in public for a couple of hours with two wet patches on the front of your blouse! All this has the very positive effect of slowing you down and keeping you around home for a few weeks, while you recuperate from the birth, and get into a rhythm with your baby and your own body. Things soon settle down, and it becomes easier (and less messy) – a natural part of the tempo of your days and nights.

> *"Incredibly, the make-up of breast milk changes to match the exact nutritional needs of a baby."*

Nature equipped women with breasts and the amazing capacity to produce living nourishment for our babies. Breastfeeding not only passes food to the baby but also immunity – something no formula is ever likely to contain. Incredibly, the make-up of breast milk changes to match the exact nutritional needs of a baby as it grows. However, women are fortunate that when breastfeeding is prevented by circumstance, substitute milk formulas are available. We urge you to maximize your chances of breastfeeding with comfort and confidence. Breastfeeding is an art, and many of us need a little help to get started. Seek information and support, such as ideas for adjustments to your feeding pattern and techniques, which will make the process pleasing and satisfying to both you and the baby. There are breastfeeding counsellors at a local level throughout the country who can be contacted by phone or in person (see p. 232). Specialists, called lactation consultants, and experienced and caring mothers offer free advice on many aspects of looking after babies. Hospital nurses and health visitors can also help to make breastfeeding easy and successful.

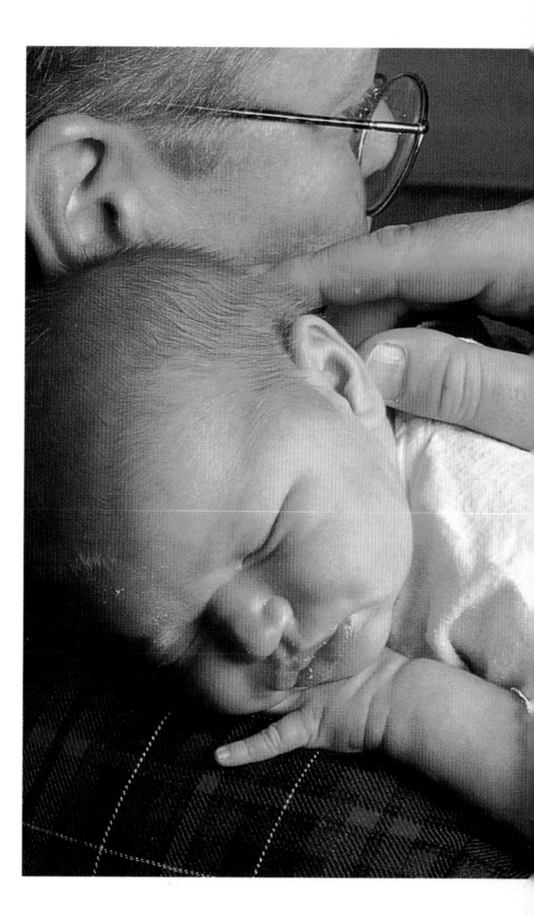

How fathers can help with breastfeeding

Fathers might feel there isn't much they can contribute to breastfeeding, but recent studies found that a dad's attitude and support do make a huge difference. If a dad knows the benefits of breastfeeding, actively helps and encourages his partner, and appreciates her commitment to breastfeeding, she is more likely to begin and continue.

Fathers can be a comfort if mothers have a difficult time with mastitis or cracked nipples, and can make sure she gets help from nursing specialists or doctors. Even when there are no problems, your partner can be useful – especially in the early weeks – by bringing the baby to you, helping you to get comfortable with cushions for back support, helping you to put your feet up, and bringing you a hot drink or a book to help you pass the time.

Opting for the bottle

If you've chosen to bottlefeed, have a talk with your midwife or health visitor about the type of formula to use, and be aware of the content of the various brands. Also ask about the different types of bottles and teats, and how to sterilize the equipment. Parents who bottlefeed can make this as near as possible to the breastfeeding experience by holding the baby close, stroking them and making lots of eye contact. The close and beautiful experience of having the baby's skin against your own bare skin is also important at least some of the time. One compensation of bottlefeeding is that both partners can be involved in sterilizing the equipment, preparing the formula and feeding the baby.

Babies are always learning

This is where it gets to be fun. There are much more interesting things you can do with babies than just feed, change, and comfort them! Babies are learning all the time. They strive to make sense of the world. Gradually, carefully, you can see them piecing things together. Where do you go when you leave the room? What is that sound coming from the box in the corner? What happens if I poke you in the eye?

They are learning to use their arms as they flap them around and bump their hands into their own faces, and stroke and prod the soft skin of your breast as they feed. Within a few weeks your baby can bring a fist to their mouth and find comfort in sucking and chomping on their own fingers.

Soon your baby can bring both hands together, and know that by aiming in a certain direction they can make the dangling toys on their pram bob and jingle. After a month or two, they will begin to show you daily advances in their communication skills. Babies placed in their cot for a nap may stiffen their limbs and wail, letting you know that sleep isn't on their agenda just now! You'll notice how babies in the bath splash carefully, so as not to wet their faces, when only weeks before they were alarming themselves with their own splashing – and bursting into tears. Just playing and responding to your baby is the best way to feed their hunger for learning.

It will help you to enjoy your child and help your child to progress, if you learn to notice little changes. Experienced parents among your friends and grandparents will often help by pointing out the baby's new skills. For instance: "Look how he knows his mother's (or father's) voice."

"Look how she turned her head to watch you go by."
"Did you hear that – That's her crabby cry – she doesn't want you to stop playing."
"She's lifting her head right up now – she didn't do that last week."
"Look, he doesn't recognize me with this sun hat on!"

Listen to what you say

When you go out with your baby in public, you will witness a very strange phenomenon. Human beings are compulsive communicators, and given a baby who is curious but wordless, they feel compelled to put extraordinary words into the infant's mouth. Have you heard this kind of thing said to babies:

★ "Isn't it a terrible world?"
★ "It's not fair, is it?"
★ "Who is this silly old lady making faces at me?"

These tell you a great deal about the adult making the statements! It's lovely that people want to talk to babies and it's very good for them. It is natural to try to imagine what the baby is thinking and feeling. Parents will watch for tiny clues in the fleeting expressions on the baby's face, the tone of their babbling, the pitch or rhythm of their cry, and their body language. We literally put words into a baby's mouth, and this is how they learn to speak and understand the world. So it pays to be aware of what you are saying. Have you ever been singing *Rock-a-bye baby* and got to the part where the bough breaks and the baby falls, and wish you hadn't started?

Since the urge is so strong to talk to babies, why not say what we really want the baby to think and feel? The power of positive suggestion is illustrated by Anna, a young mother who wrote to us after reading our book *The Secret of Happy Children*, and told us her story:

> *As the mother of a three-month-old baby, I was very distraught. The baby was hard to comfort, everyone else seemed good at it except me, and I was feeling so tired and depressed. Someone gave me your book and I read about "Seeds in the Mind" – what you say to your children. I listened to what I was saying to little Angie at odd times during the day. I was horrified. I heard myself say, "You're a real little bitch, aren't you?", when she spat out some milk. "You know I'm a hopeless mother, don't you?" "Nothing I do makes you happy, does it?" – stuff like that. I resolved there and then to change what came out of my mouth. I'll never know if she changed first or if it was a change in me, but Angie became easier to handle almost from that day onwards.*
>
> *I think the change was in me as well, and she was getting a nicer feeling from me that made the difference. I wasn't talking to her like she was an enemy.*
>
> ***Anna, 42***

We were troubled one day when we saw a new mother in a health centre waiting room, proudly holding her tiny, exquisite baby daughter, saying, "You're a rotten little tramp, aren't you? Yes, just a rotten little tramp!" – all this said with a warm and pleasant voice. This mother loved and was proud of her baby, but was unable to say it straight out. She would not really want her child to grow up and believe such messages.

There's another neat trick you can try. Since no-one really has a clue what a baby is thinking, we may as well have positive fantasies! If your child is two months old and continually crying and colicky, try telling yourself that they are really saying, "Thank you for putting up with me, I'll be eternally grateful to you." This cry-interpretation became a joke in our family. Woken in the early hours, we would translate full-voiced bawling into, "I don't mean to upset you. Thanks for giving up your sleep to show me how important I am to you. I think you're a beautiful mother, Mum. I just want to check that you are still there."

Playing with babies

For a long time while they are growing, babies don't give us much back. They can't actually say, "Thanks" or "Nice nappy change there". It takes a couple of months before they even smile. Babies can't give us a present or bring us a cup of tea. The best way to get reward from our babies is to have fun with them. They will be responsive and show enjoyment as soon as we put in some energy to smile, touch and talk to them. There are two secrets of play with babies:

★ keep it simple and gentle
★ use lots of repetition.

Keeping it simple

Games start with very simple things done over and over. If the baby sneezes, you exclaim with a smile, "You sneezed!" Your child, unsure how to feel, decides this is a happy thing and smiles back! Soon they will look to your face expectantly after every sneeze and smile in anticipation. This can lead you on to simple games, like taking your baby's little fist and patting it against their nose and saying, "Nose, nose, nose." Then you can pat your baby's cheek, saying, "Cheek, cheek, cheek." This certainly can bring out a new side of you. If you sound like a happy lunatic you are probably getting it right! Our local plumber, Dave, was worried that his nine-month-old

Good things to try

Disappearing games

These are games where things or people go out of sight, and then magically reappear. Disappearing games seem to be vital for babies in learning that things or people go away but will come back.

Babies don't understand how time and space work. So, if they see you go out of the room, they may cry, thinking you are gone forever. For them, the present is all there is. Gradually, they figure out that you will come back. Peek-a-boo games help them to make this connection.

★ ***Try hiding your eyes behind your hands and saying,*** *"Where's Mummy?"* Then move your hands down and say, *"Boo! Here I am!"* You can do this while your baby is in her highchair, or while she is lying on her back, bright and alert after a nappy change.

★ ***Lift up your baby's feet and legs to hide your face,*** lower them again and say, *"Boo!"* Or drop a scarf over her head and let her pull if off. Also let your baby pull a scarf off your face and head, and laugh and smile as you emerge.

★ ***Hide a favourite toy under a clean nappy that's within your baby's reach,*** so that she looks for it and finds it underneath. Older brothers and sisters can play these games as their special contribution. They will often have more time and patience, and love to make the baby laugh by creating variations of each hiding game.

"Where's Mummy?"

"Here I am!"

"Peek-a-boo!"

wouldn't learn to crawl, so he got down on the floor and gave his baby lessons until he got the idea! We'd love to have got it on video!

When you change your baby's clothes, take time to blow raspberries and hum against the skin of their tummy. Babies love it all – the closeness, the vibration and the chance to grab a handful of your hair. Tap their feet together, kiss the soles of their feet, sing a song. Enjoy yourselves.

Repeating it again and again

Babies will also play repetition games with you (whether you like it or not!) and they are right into cause and effect. So the combination works something like this:"If I drop this toy over the edge of the pram, it will disappear, but make a noise, and then I will call out and you will come and it will reappear, and then I can do it all again. Whoopee!"

They squeal, you pick them up. They point to their mouths, you feed them. They reach up from their cots, you take them in your arms and hug them. They smile, and people smile back. This is the foundation of self-esteem: "I can affect the world and the way it treats me."

You don't have to respond every time. They will learn that "You don't always get what you want when you want it", but they have enough success to feel that life is pretty good and everything is "under control".

Human beings learn by repeating things over and over until we get them right. Babies are self-programmed to learn and so they love repetition and familiarity, with just a bit of surprise thrown in. Watch as you start to play a game – your baby's whole body starts to dance and sway with delight at the rhythm of your voice as you repeat a familiar rhyme or sequence, and add little variations.

The first game that I made up which really made my baby laugh was this one. I would lie her on the floor on her back, and sit in front of her. I'd hold my hands out in front of me, and say, "Tickle, tickle" and I'd slowly move them closer till I got to her chest, where I'd tickle her. Now she is laughing and giggling even before I get there. So I sometimes stop all of a sudden and she looks for where the tickling has gone – and I bring the hands back all of a sudden and she is laughing again. You just make it up as you go along, and bring in changes to surprise them.

Sandy, 19

It's rougher with dad

Dads will often play with babies in much more vigorous and adventurous ways. When they do it's important to take notice of your child's reaction, not your own. We watched a dad in a doctor's waiting room whose baby was lying on the carpeted floor in front of him. The baby kept slowly struggling over to him, at which point the dad would push the baby back gently with his foot to where he had started from. The baby had to start all over again, but never once cried. Babies often love the way dads play with them.

A change of identity

It takes a little while for some mothers and fathers to loosen up about play, especially to take time out from rushing to do household chores, community involvements or work. Perhaps you are used to doing "productive" things like going to meetings, writing letters, making sales, and so on. Or perhaps you are the height of domestic efficiency, so that just spending a languid afternoon with your baby makes you feel guilty. All we can say is – forget it. You are teaching one of the few human beings who will be entirely trusted to you how to laugh, learn, and love people. There is nothing more worthwhile that you will ever do.

parents deserve a better world

What sort of a world do we want to live in? Much of the world around us is dirty, dangerous and stupid – the very opposite of how it should be for us to do our job of raising kids. You are never more acutely aware of this than when you hold your helpless, innocent baby in your arms and contemplate the conditions they must grow up in.

Imagine for a minute what the world would be like if it was designed to be a good place for parents and children. It would be a very different place. We would live in smaller communities, with lots of connections between the ages, from respected and cared for old people through to newborns.

Families would have privacy without isolation. There would be quiet, friendly, simple housing, in safe, car-free precincts. There would be gathering places like community gardens, parks, neighbourhood centres, and pleasant places to walk, shop, and meet. Celebrations – like festivals, picnics, plantings, fairs and cultural events – would bring families together to enjoy each other and the place they live in.

Schools would have mothers, fathers and grandparents visiting, reading, encouraging and helping. Parents could take their children to work sometimes (maybe often) and work would have flexible hours to match schooling and family responsibilities and health needs. The younger the child, the more financial and community support would be provided, lessening the economic pressures on parents so they could participate in their child's precious early years.

People, valuing the job of parents, would practice patience and compassion. They'd always offer help to the mother struggling with a pusher trying to climb onto a bus and to the father with three bags of groceries, juggling a squirming toddler at the supermarket door.

Local shopkeepers, banks and doctors' surgeries would know you and your children by name, and have toy corners where children are welcome to entertain themselves while you are there. When word gets out that someone is sick, casseroles would arrive at your door with a warm "get well" card attached. When gardens are abundant, surplus organic fruit and vegetables would be shared with young families. When financial loss or disaster occurred, the "hat" would be passed around and filled to help you get back on your feet.

Sharing resources would be an everyday event. There would be free toy libraries. Childhood gear, like prams, clothes, books, toys and car seats, would be pooled and recycled. We would have affordable and reliable public transport. Cars or minibuses would be share-owned for use when you needed them. People would look out for each other. A child in distress or heading towards danger would be attended to by the nearest adult or older child.

People would be friendly to teenagers and show an interest in teaching them; and would make them feel welcome when things are a bit tense at home. Adults would also keep an eye out and intervene thoughtfully when teenagers were acting in risky or foolish ways. There would be great youth groups run by young adults and older people. In each community, you would find lots of sports, activities and learning of every kind, for every age group.

Take heart, therefore, if being a parent sometimes seems impossibly hard – don't always blame yourself. Think how much easier parenting would be if friendship, community and happiness were the national priorities instead of money and power. The world we have described above may seem impossibly utopian, and yet every one of these ideas is being achieved by people in some part of the world today. In fact, you can begin today to live your life more along these lines. By working with others, you can begin to gradually change local, and one day global, conditions for families.

chapter 4

the mobile baby

Rhythms of life

By the time your child is crawling, you will be a much more experienced parent – having had months of practice. By now you will have discovered some distinctive patterns in your baby's day. There is often one longer sleep (hopefully at night time). There will be times of the day when your baby seems particularly happy and active, and other times when they are more prone to being upset or irritable.

Each baby's patterns are unique and sometimes, when you think you've figured them out, they change and you have to think again! But don't despair – after a few months you get to know how long your baby can stay awake before needing another nap, the average length of nap periods, and how many they'll have in a day and when and how often they need a feed.

Julia's pattern

Little Julia, at seven months:

- wakes between 6.30 and 7 am
- is fed breakfast, dressed and plays until about 10 am
- sleeps for 30–45 minutes
- is up again at about 11 am, then changed, played with and fed lunch
- has an afternoon nap of 30–60 minutes at about 2 or 3 pm
- may have a short nap at 6 pm
- between 6 to 7.30 pm she has her evening meal, and a bath with her Dad
- has her evening breastfeed and goes off to bed at 8 pm.

Overnight, Julia will wake once or twice for a quick breastfeed. Her parents keep the room dark so she doesn't wake up too much and think it's playtime! They use a thick, double nappy at night time to avoid having to change her as well. Because she sleeps in a cot at their

bedside, they can easily lift her into bed, and she doesn't get lonely or cry or fuss. At 6.30 am the day starts again, and she won't be fooled into going back to sleep.

Ben's pattern

Julia's cousin, Ben, is eight months old, and he has slept 10 hours a night, every night, since birth, with two long naps in the day as well. (Don't you just wish you had a baby like this?) Another child at the same health clinic as Ben had been waking for a feed every two hours, 24 hours a day, for the first 10 months! Then, within the space of a week, he grew his fourth tooth, refused the breast and began sleeping through the night! No two babies, even twins, have identical patterns – they are all different.

"Are you receiving me, over?"

You will learn to easily distinguish between the crying sounds your baby makes to let you know that they are:

★ hurt (from banging their head on something)
★ angry (because someone has taken a toy away)
★ hungry
★ tired.

You will be forming a clearer picture of this baby's personality. This new individual already shows distinct tendencies towards being peaceful and placid, or alert and active, or friendly and co-operative. Babies are each so different – some prefer people, some prefer toys, some are adaptable, while others are sensitive and easily upset.

By the time babies are up and crawling about, they are no longer sponge-like newborn infants soaking up the world. They are starting to show their preferences. If you can figure out your baby's needs, then it helps you to plan for an easy time. You may decide that the camping trip around Australia had better wait a year!

The intrepid explorer

Here they go, off and about – looking, touching, grabbing and tasting, dropping, banging and getting to know everything within reach. At the same time, babies are getting to know their own bodies and how to make them

Good things to try

Entertaining your baby

There are times when a baby will get bored or impatient if expected to sit still – in a queue, on a bus, at the doctor's. Remember that babies love some action and you can have fun with them almost anywhere... *Tickles! Peek-a-boo!* Hiding behind a couch or door and jumping out; tugging their clothes; making funny faces or sounds; using your hands like puppets; letting them pull your hat off and looking dismayed; holding one of their hands, pushing it on your nose and saying, "*Beep, beep!*". Laying them on the floor on their back and dropping a small soft toy onto their tummies; blowing raspberries onto their skin; looking into a mirror together; pointing out any cat or dog or animal in view – and whatever else you can think of!

This Little Piggy

For generations, parents have played this toe game. While holding up your baby's foot for them to see, you recite the words, while taking each toe in turn and wiggling it around.

This little piggy went to market,
This little piggy stayed at home,
This little piggy had roast beef,
This little piggy had none,
This little piggy went wee wee wee wee all the way home.

(During the last line, run your fingers up your baby's leg and under their armpit for an exciting burst of tickling!)

Hair sweeping

Babies often like to feel your hair on their skin; try sweeping their tummy with it to bring giggles of pleasure.

The teddy bear game

This great tickle game starts with you circling your finger in the palm of your baby's hand.

Round and round the garden,
Like a teddy bear,
One step ('walking' two fingers up their arm),
Two steps (moving your fingers closer to their armpit),
Tickle you under there (running your fingers to their armpit or under their chin for a last big tickle).

work. Many hours are spent practising new skills – newly mobile babies will rock on all fours, so only their hands and feet are on the ground, and delight in arching their back and looking through their legs.

Later they will insist on being helped to stand, and will grasp both your hands as supports, and make you walk with them as they totter along. Before long they will pull themselves up to standing position using the front of a couch, then clamber onto vacuum cleaners and low tables. Mobile babies will enjoy slapping their hands on top of the cushions as they creep along the edge of chairs and other furniture. They love it when you encourage them. If they hear appreciative noises, they will stop, look back and smile proudly.

Safe and sound

Mobile babies can roll, crawl, topple, walk or just drag themselves along. Babies become mobile at different rates – it's not a race. Each will do it in their own time. Sometimes it happens suddenly. One day you may leave your baby on the floor to kick their legs while you fetch a fresh nappy and return to find them under the table four metres away, sucking a chair leg. It can be quite a jolt to realize your baby is on the move!

Having a mobile baby means everything has to change around the house. No longer can you leave a heater turned on in the corner of the room, as your baby can now get over to it in a flash. What used to look like a clean floor, on close inspection renders up dead flies for sucking, coins for swallowing, pins and open staples for bare knees to catch on, loose plugs and wires for little fingers to pry into and newspapers for mushing to a pulp with little gums. Your lounge room has become a sensory wonderland! You literally need a floor you could eat off, because that's what your baby will do!

Taking precautions

Some people recommend that you check for possible hazards by crawling around your house looking at it from a baby's angle. A group of parents we asked suggested the following safety measures:

- ★ move or change electric kettle cords that hang down within reach
- ★ store any dangerous substances safely out of reach – for example, cleaning fluids, detergents, medicines, pesticides and other poisons, or any other chemicals – even vitamins and herbal preparations. Either install cupboard locks or remove the items from low cupboards and put them away in boxes, out of reach of growing children. In fact, sort through and decide if you can do without a lot of the household chemicals you use
- ★ put gates or barriers across the top or bottom of stairs
- ★ keep your baby's highchair in an open area out of reach of benches
- ★ keep fans and fan heaters out of reach
- ★ always stay close when your baby is eating, and cut food into small pieces to reduce the risk of choking
- ★ check for any furniture, such as lamps and bookshelves, that your baby could pull over
- ★ install plastic safety covers in unused electrical outlets, or have an electrician fit an earth leakage circuit breaker which helps prevent electrocution in the whole house
- ★ inspect toys for small parts that could be swallowed, or sharp edges and moving parts that might trap little fingers
- ★ be aware that toy boxes with heavy lids are a danger, as are piano lids
- ★ be alert with a baby who is in the bath, as they will start to lunge and slip about more and may try to turn on the taps. *Never* leave a baby in the bath even for a moment. If the phone or doorbell rings, ignore it, or take your baby with you
- ★ put screens around woodfires and heaters

- ★ tie up plastic shopping bags in a knot before you store them, to prevent suffocation
- ★ throw away plastic ties or clips from bread bags – they are a choking hazard
- ★ ensure that any beanbags aren't leaking – if the beans spill out, they can be inhaled and cause choking or lung problems
- ★ start good habits – don't let your baby play with matches, lighters, electrical cords, power outlets, appliances or taps
- ★ remove ashtrays and their contents from reach
- ★ watch routes taken by people with hot drinks or pans, who could trip over a lunging tot in their path (waiters in restaurants are often not alert to babies – they count on customers being still as they juggle and deliver hot dishes and drinks)
- ★ close swimming-pool gates; cover ponds and waterbutts, and never leave your baby unsupervised near a swimming pool.

These are just some examples of possible hazards. There are many other things that apply in your particular environment – just look around and check. It helps to remind yourself that you need to be alert and vigilant now, whenever your little one is up and about. It soon becomes second nature to look ahead, and to check that the floor looks safe and an activity can't hurt them. You'll notice that other parents of mobile babies are good at this as well. Start noticing little details. People who haven't had children around for a while don't tend to foresee the danger in everyday things, such as leaving hot drinks on low tables.

Always have an adult in charge

Other children can be a great source of entertainment and amusement for your mobile baby, but they cannot and should not be expected to be in charge of safety. An adult should always be in charge of a baby's safety and should provide constant supervision all the time the baby is awake.

If one adult needs to leave the room for a while to do the washing, cook a meal, or go out, another adult must take over the "watching" of the baby. We call this the "hand over". One parent asks the other to watch the baby while they are busy and when they return, they clearly say, "I'll take over again now." Obviously, if both of you are around the baby, both will be responsible for

watching. Many times when something happens and a child is hurt, it's because one parent thought the other was watching – they hadn't been clear.

As your child grows older there will be more and more safe opportunities for unsupervised play. With practice, parents develop unexpected skills – the "Parent's Ear" can hear:

★ the quietness of mischief
★ the distinct sucking sound of a fly being savoured
★ the quick gulp that means, "Too late" – it's gone down the hatch!

"Parental Intuition" develops, whereby parents become inexplicably uncomfortable about their child being with certain people, or they may feel a sudden urge to go and check the baby. For every 40 times you act on this intuition, with no apparent need, there will be that one time that makes it worthwhile.

> *"As children grow, they can learn to feel proud of being safe, rather than always fearful of danger."*

How to teach babies to stay away from danger

You can make your home safer, but you can't cocoon your children, so you have to teach them to stay safe as they grow older. If a child is heading for, or playing with, a dangerous object, act first. Pick the child up, or pull their hands away, and say in a serious voice, "Come away" "Hot! Hands off!" This is deliberately worded, to tell the child what to do, as opposed to what not to do. Take the child away and give them something to play with.

As children learn to understand speech, they will automatically think "hands off" or "stay away". This is much more useful than what people often say – "Don't touch it or you'll burn yourself", which can plant the image in a child's mind of the bad outcome, and may make them fascinated with doing it. Be firm and stay stern!

Although it's entertaining to watch babies determinedly trying to get back to the power socket time and again, and you can't help but admire their spirit, resist the temptation to laugh. Tell your partner about it and have a laugh later. A baby could think, "Oh goody – this is a game", and mischievously grin and head back in the same direction. It wouldn't be funny if they did hurt themselves, so take it seriously.

For babies, the whole world is of interest. They grab a shiny toy, which happens to be a sharp knife. They don't know it's wrong. You know that they have to be stopped, and that smacking or shaking will only inflict pain that they can't understand, or do real damage, which is what you were wanting to prevent in the first place. Babies are not naughty, they just don't understand. When you take a stand, you act without blame. You are saying by your actions, "You are precious. This is a limit I won't let you cross." These are the seeds of discipline.

As kids grow older, more explanations can be used, and you can even allow them to hurt themselves a little so that they can see the consequences of their own actions.

In short, to keep mobile babies safe, you need to:

★ organize their physical environment
★ keep them under constant supervision
★ act to rescue them from danger
★ start to teach them self-control.

As children grow, they can learn to feel proud of being safe, rather than always fearful of danger.

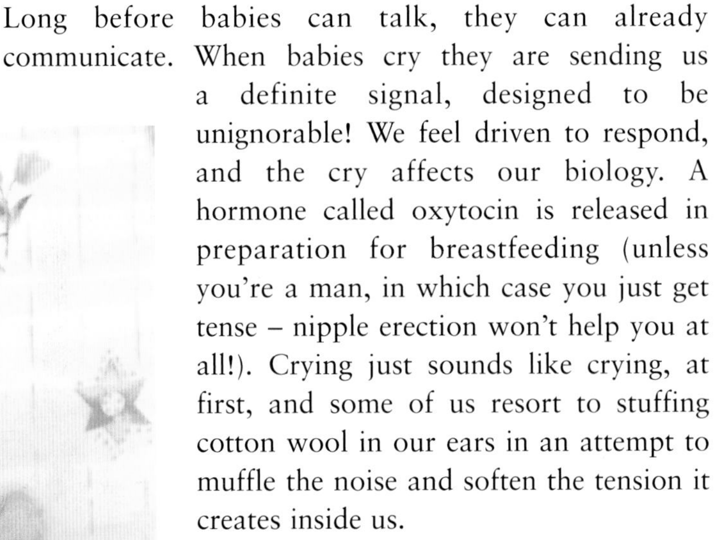

Communication techniques

Long before babies can talk, they can already communicate. When babies cry they are sending us a definite signal, designed to be unignorable! We feel driven to respond, and the cry affects our biology. A hormone called oxytocin is released in preparation for breastfeeding (unless you're a man, in which case you just get tense – nipple erection won't help you at all!). Crying just sounds like crying, at first, and some of us resort to stuffing cotton wool in our ears in an attempt to muffle the noise and soften the tension it creates inside us.

In traditional societies, babies rarely cried – their needs were always taken care of immediately, they were continually "in arms" and were remarkably placid. Hunter-gatherer tribes in all corners of the world still have this ability to keep babies happy. Prolonged crying in nature usually means a baby is in distress, and a part of us gets very worked up with the sound. Perhaps this is the adrenaline we would need if we had to fight to protect our babies!

Babytalk

You will begin to recognize slightly different tones and tempos in your baby's cries. For instance, a hungry cry might sound more forceful and urgent – as compared to the weaker, lower-pitched, broken or repetitive cries of the tired baby before they fall asleep. Don't be concerned if it all just sounds the same to you. You will eventually know for sure the difference between a sharp cry of pain and a complaint that sounds grizzly, but not distressed. If you try taking a toy away from a mobile baby, you can

Good things to try

Being pushed to your limits

Most parents, at some time or another, will have violent thoughts towards their baby. Often the reason is just the sheer stress of fatigue and feeling of failure after "trying everything" to soothe a fretful infant. If you were often hit as a child, you may be more prone to violent feelings under stress. Also, if you are unwell, or over-tired, or if you have marriage or money worries, you are much more likely to feel distressed. So take extra care at these times.

All parents need a plan in case they find themselves desperate enough to feel they want to hit their child. These are what worked for us – you might want to add your own:

★ ***put the baby somewhere safe*** – usually in a cot

★ ***leave the room*** and go somewhere quieter in the house

★ ***decide what you need to do*** to release your feelings – if you feel like screaming but are too embarrassed, scream into a pillow! If you feel like hitting out, hit a bed or some soft furniture. Try to rip up a thick blanket or chomp it with your teeth. Run cold water over your face and hands. Drink some water. Sit down and slow your breathing. Cry. Have a cup of tea, read the paper, listen to music. Some parents keep a photo of their child looking really cute or happy, and look at this to regain their sense of perspective.

★ ***get some human support*** if you need it. Ring someone up – a friend or a health visitor. Ring a parent help line for support (see p. 232). If you are having these feelings more than just occasionally, take some time to seek experienced help. All parents need help sometimes.

imagine the reaction. The cry is like a car with a battery problem. It ticks over slowly – Aaah, Aaah, Aaah! The lip drops. Then it roars into action: WaaAAAAGHhh, WaaAAAAGHhh!

Learning language

As babies learn to eat solid food, their tongues and mouths get better at producing interesting sounds. It's about this time that they all start to babble. They also

gurgle, blow raspberries, and say simple words like "Mum-Mum" and "Dad-Dad". Learning to speak is like learning a song – you get the tune first, then you learn the words. Even in the womb, the baby is surrounded by the lilting flow of language. As soon as you feel like it, talk and read stories to your baby. Tiny babies will watch your face and the movement of the pages; they will start to see the pictures and enjoy hearing you making exaggerated sound effects. Books made in a small size with thick pages, bright pictures and short sentences are great.

Babies will soon learn that the noises they make interest you as well. Each time a child gets you to understand them, they feel powerful and confident. Watch a grandparent with a littlie who is making noises at them, and hear the grandparent pretending to converse: "How are you darling?", "Gaaaruhgggh", "Is that right?", "Dagooooooo", "Oh, I see!". The child will continue earnestly with the conversation – a flow of bubbling sounds – in response to the rewarding feedback.

Sign language

Babies can talk with their bodies. Most of it is pretty obvious, some you have to look for. If you hold a baby, and they squirm and arch their back making their legs slide down, it's likely they want to be put down.

If they crawl over, grab your leg, look up at you and cry, perhaps they want to be picked up. If they are crying and you hand them a biscuit, which they immediately sling across the room, that probably wasn't what they wanted!

When you pick them up and they start to bang on your chest, pull on your clothes, and bury their head into you, maybe it's time for a breastfeed.

There is no mistaking the "baby smooch" where they gently lean their forehead into your cheek, or give you a "kiss" with an open mouth and wet pulsating tongue on your face. Some of the signs a baby makes are more subtle, using small movements of fingers, hands and feet.

When her big brother starts crawling behind the couch, seven-month-old Jenny's feet start to jump up and down. She's excited. She knows it's hide-and-seek time. If Jenny spots the bottle being carried towards her, and she is hungry, she will slap a hand up and down on her side. She's ready to go for it! You'll also know Jenny is hungry when she sticks a finger in the side of her mouth. This means – put it here. She also chews her fist.

If you see a baby staring at a toy, watch to see if their hand is opening and closing. If so, try placing the toy into their hand, then watch the response. A baby will soon let you know that they are pleased you understood – they will smile and do it again.

As babies get to know certain routines, like bathing, they begin to anticipate the event – for example, when they see the bath running, they will pull at their clothes. This is their way of showing you that they are expecting their clothes to be coming off.

Your baby will have their own special signs, which you as the parent will notice first, because you are most attuned to them, and to the fine details of their sounds and actions. Your responses will make your child confident in their first steps to reach out and communicate.

How kids learn to talk

As soon as a child is born, they make noises – but that's all. Yet, by five, they can speak clearly and follow complex rules of grammar without even knowing it. This is a miracle. But it's a miracle that you can help along.

All stages differ with the individual, and also boys are usually a little slower than girls. So don't treat this as more than a rough guide. Having said that, if you are worried that your child is way behind, it may be worth having their hearing checked and, if that's not the problem, talk to a speech therapist to see if help is needed.

★ **0–3 months**

Baby learns that you can get attention by making unhappy noises. People come and do stuff to make you feel better. Then you feel better and make happy noises. This makes everyone happy.

★ **3–6 months**

They can laugh, chuckle, squeal and even scream if something annoys them. They makes sounds like ah ah, moo moo, goo, derr, aroo, and take great pleasure in repeating these to themselves in their cots. They don't seem to understand words yet, but they understand the tone of your voice.

★ **6–9 months**

They listen to conversations and join in with babbling – dadada and gagaga and mamamamam. Parents listen and repeat back words they think they recognize. "Mama" and "Dada" go down especially well. They will understand "no", and "bye-bye" though they can't say these yet.

★ **9–12 months**

They will know and recognize their name and turn and smile if they hear it. They will *understand* several words like cup, teddy, pussy, car (though probably not yet speak them). And they will carry out simple instructions if you do the gestures to help them – "Give it to Daddy", "Say bye-bye", "Can you cook dinner tonight?" (I made the last one up. Sorry!).

★ **12–15 months**

It is likely that they will now use their first real words (apart from Mummy and Daddy) and may soon be pointing to things and saying what they are. They will understand "Give me the ball", "Kiss mummy goodnight!", "Don't touch".

★ **15–18 months**

They may be able to say up to 20 words, and understand nearly 100. They will be very chatty, and like looking at picture books and naming things. They will repeat the last word of things you say: "Want to go to the garden?" – "Garden!"

★ **1½–2 years**

They will talk in long sentences to themselves which no-one else will understand! (Kind of like a computer salesman.) If their parents or brothers and sisters talk to them, they will progress a lot quicker. They can make combinations of words all their own:"More cake!", "Daddy gone!". They will love songs and nursery rhymes.

★ **2–2½ years**
They give running commentaries to themselves as they play, and use sentences almost like adult sentences. They even change their voice like a ventriloquist to make their different animals talk – teddy, rabbit, doggy. They ask endless questions – "Why?" "Who?" "What?" – and you have to be patient in trying to give answers. They will love listening to stories from a book, and will notice the words on the page. They are getting the message that it's fun to read, especially on someone's comfortable lap.

★ **2½–3 years**
They will have hundreds of words, and speak very well – "The tricycle's got wet." They can count, but don't really understand numbers – it's just a rhyme to them.

★ **3–4 years**
They can discuss so well, strangers will have conversations with them. They make "mistakes", showing that they are building up their own grammar system: "I buyed a lickle car yesterday", "My ball is more bigger than yours". No need to correct them, they will eventually notice and copy your speech more closely, provided you simply confirm that you have understood what they meant by saying it in the correct way. They can also play funny word games: "One two, buckle my sock; three, four, knock at the gate!" and think these are very hilarious.

★ **4–5 years**
By now they will have grasped the basic grammatical patterns, but they will still be showing creative use of language: "We're having a hamburglar for tea", "Where did you went Mummy?", "I'm all fused up" (confused and fed up). The best way that you can help is by making everyday situations a chance to chat happily with your child.

We are grateful for the material on this page to Mr. Peter Downes, a modern language consultant in Cambridgeshire, England.

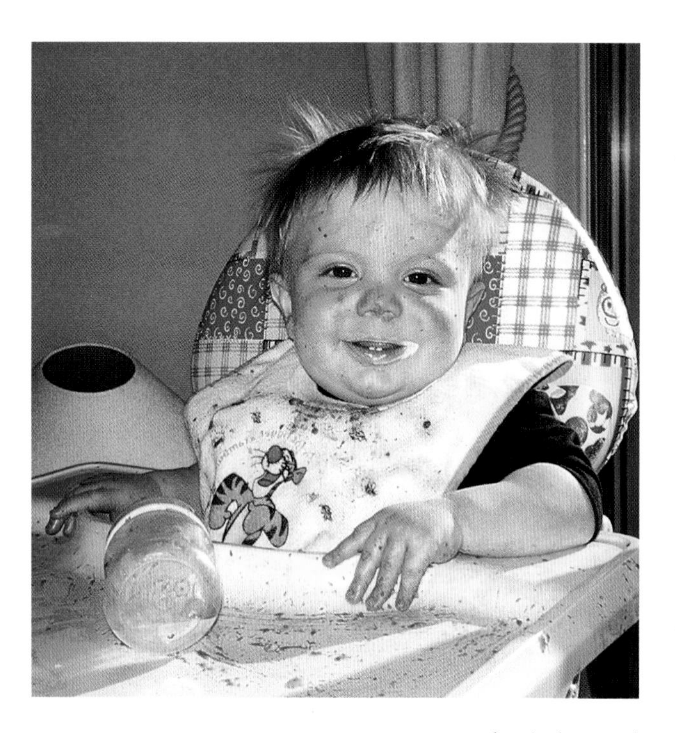

Growing competence

As their first birthday approaches, most babies are taking solid food, and drinking from bottles or cups. They are becoming more a part of the normal family activities – instead of the family revolving around them. Even their diet is less special and they may even handle small amounts of what the family is eating.

As babies begin to eat solids, they will naturally reach for the spoon, and help the food to be put in their mouths (or on their hair or clothes!). They will also grab and control their own cups and bottles, and pick up small pieces of soft food, and feed themselves. As your child learns to feed themselves, their confidence and contentment grows. It's a great plus for parents too!

These accomplishments continue, with sitting up, crawling, creeping and walking, and playing contentedly on their own (for up to 15 seconds!).

At this age your baby may crawl speedily after you as you go from room to room, and cry with annoyance if you go too fast!

Trust through familiarity

After a while, routines will start to "make sense" to your baby and they will be anticipating what comes next. For instance, at six months of age, little Tamara hated her car seat. Strapping her in would bring howls of protest.

Now, aged one, the mention of "School", "Car" and "Brother", in any order, magically removes the fuss, because she looks forward to getting her brother from school in the car. Having rituals and order in your daily life will help your baby "know where they are" and build up a sense of trust. Their relationships with others are strengthening now. They love familiar faces and places.

Good things to try

Birthday letters

A woman once related a beautiful story to us about her father. She had experienced many problems with him, both when she was growing up and as an adult. Even after his death, she had unresolved feelings.

Then she discovered a letter he had written to her when she was only one year old. It accompanied a teddy bear and now, at 40, she treasures the bear and the letter because she really didn't know until then that her father had loved her and felt so gently towards her. Since hearing this story, we have written (and kept in a safe place) yearly birthday letters that describe to our children what is happening in their lives at the time of their birthday – their achievements, likes, dislikes and special events.

Here's an example:

Happy first birthday!

Right now you are a beautiful, black-haired, brown-eyed boy. You have a delightful giggle, and burst into raucous laughter, especially when tickled or chased down the hallway.

You spend lots of time with your wooden blocks and outside in the garden, where you pull up carrots and wash them in the wheelbarrow.

You love stories of all shapes and sizes and amazed us by bringing a brick into the house the other day.

On the difficult side, you wriggle and squirm and cry about getting changed.

Today, you discovered noses, and pointed to mine, yours and even the man on TV's nose.

Up on their own two feet

One day soon your baby will take their first amazing steps on their own two feet – their baby days will be coming to an end and toddlerhood beginning. As you look back on all that your baby has learned in these first months, you will be amazed and proud.

Through care, physical endurance and loving attention to detail, you have brought your baby safely through their most dependent time. What an achievement! Go and buy yourself a present. You deserve it.

chapter 5

toddlers!!

Stepping into a new stage of life

Two- to three-year-old children are justifiably proud of themselves. They can make their legs move them to where they want to go. (That's what toddler means, after all – someone who can toddle along.) They can reach things, copy other people and almost feed themselves. They can tell you where it hurts. They can put on and take off some of their clothes. They know where the good things to eat are, and how to get at them.

There's something else pretty big happening at this age – words. Toddlers can usually get you to understand what they want. They have learned some powerful words like, "Hungry", "Drink", "Potty", "Thank you (Sank-you!)", "Please (pease!)", "Mine!". They certainly know "Yes" and "No". You could probably get by in a foreign country if you knew these few toddler words!

Parents love to hear these words – especially "Thank you", "Please" and "Yes". It's good to know when they are "Hungry" or "Thirsty" without first having to be cried to or screeched at. And we are "tickled pink" when they say "Potty" or "Toilet" and will move mountains immediately such words are mentioned.

"No", however, is a harder word to take, for both parents and toddlers. Even as adults we find it a difficult word to use. Many of us can't seem to say "No" to other people, or we feel guilty if we do. Often we try to find nicer words like, "Thank you so much but unfortunately I am unable ..." or "I would love to – let me get back to you." If we're honest, we don't like to be on the receiving end when "No" is said to us either.

"Can you come and fix my car?"–"No."
"Do you like my mother?" – "No."
"Would you like to come up for coffee?"– "No."
"Don't you care?" – "No."

Can you feel the sinking in your gut, the slight contraction of your chest – like a flinch – the tightening of your throat? We all experience it uniquely but, at best, hearing a "No" is a flat, stopping sort of feeling.

The world of the toddler has lots of "No's" in it. Babies usually get a "yes" from us because what they want is simple – food, comfort, loving touch. But toddlers want the world! They want you to open the icecream store just for them. They want to play in the traffic. They want to post sliced bread into the front of your video. It's hard for them, having once been the centre of the universe, to suddenly be frustrated in their wants.

Learning about early discipline

There's no doubt that the biggest difficulty parents have with toddlers is getting them to co-operate. The big challenge is to somehow take this boisterous "I want it now" little person and, without crushing their spirit with fear or humiliation, help them learn to stay out of danger, avoid trouble and get along with others.

What should you do when children act "naughty"? How can we get them to stop hitting other children, making a big mess, refusing to co-operate? Children need boundaries, but how do we set these? We don't want to go back to the old ways of hitting, yelling and calling kids names. The good news is – you don't have to. The true meaning of discipline is teaching. It means helping your child find a better way. Here is how to go about it...

It's our loving relationship with children that makes it possible to guide them to better behaviour.

Drawing on a fund of trust

The beginning of discipline training is not at two, but at birth. It's our loving relationship with our children that makes it possible to guide them to better behaviour. By helping them with their needs from the very first moment, you have built up a "trust fund", a trusting relationship in which they have learned that you are deeply committed to their interests. Think of how many times a day you helped your child during the mobile baby stage. You have soothed their hurts, kissed it better, eased their hunger, come when they called. You've explained what loud noises are: "It's okay, the bus makes that SHHH sound when it stops"; "That dog is barking because he doesn't know us". In a hundred different ways you have proven yourself to your baby. This means that when the time comes to influence or direct a baby or child away from harm or problems, you have a lot of credit. They trust you as their interpreter and go-between with the big world, and they know you help make good things happen. It's the history of loving interaction that makes a child more able to take direction from you. (That's why a step-parent or someone who adopts a toddler must first build up a relationship before they start disciplining.)

Without even realizing it, all through the mobile baby stage, you have been guiding your baby away from trouble and towards safety and enjoyment. You have been exerting all kinds of teaching and discipline without calling it by that name. Now, as the toddler stage begins, and the child develops an even stronger sense of self, you

Good things to try

The stop game

A child's ability to stop abruptly, on command, can be life saving. Every parent has needed to call a child to halt as they run towards traffic or other unseen danger.

You can start teaching a comfortable acceptance of the "Stop" word with a very young child.

★ ***With an infant***, you begin with any fun thing they are doing. Join in the activity with them, then say "Stop" and stop them with your hands. For example, in the bath, or pool, both of you slap the water – splash, splash, splash – then say "Stop", holding their hands still. Repeat the game.

★ ***Say "Good stopping"***, when they do it by themselves. You could swing them around you and say "Stop", then swing them until they say "Stop" and you obey. Later, they can run on the spot, until you say "Stop". Build up to having them stop when they are running forwards.

★ ***With older children***, include an explanation of its importance. You can also correct them if they are slow in responding, by instructing them: "When I say "Stop", you should do it straight away. Start again and show me how you do it straight away. That's right."

★ ***Benefits***: This game helps children learn an automatic reaction that might be life-saving. By learning in a playful way, with the reward of encouragement, there is built-in pleasure and a feeling of achievement.

still build on this principle of helping them learn the right way to go, but add on new strategies to take advantage of their growing skills.

The first thing is to match your methods to their age and ability. Just as there's no point in lecturing a two-month-old about germs, a six-year-old needs more than to be told, "Yukky! Hands off that part of the dog."

There are three stages of discipline that parents can use which take account of children's gradually growing ability to understand. These are:

1 Distracting
2 Redirecting
3 The teaching conversation.

These are respectful ways that keep conflict to a minimum and help your child learn self control of their feelings, thoughts and actions.

The three stages of discipline

1 Distracting babies

A little baby can usually be distracted away from something you don't want them to do. It they are unhappy or frustrated, they can usually be picked up, cuddled, taken outside or given a toy. They are usually quick to forget the problem and are soon happy again. Skilful or experienced parents are forever diverting their babies – for example, to keep them from getting bored on a bus ride they might occupy them with a set of keys to jingle or point out "Look at the doggy".

The older mobile babies get though, the harder they are to distract. They get fixed on the object of their desire and won't give up. Their body language shows their displeasure – if they are not impressed, they screech, grab, scratch, kick, drop down to the ground and burst into

Good things to try

The toddler test

The toddler years test you quite a lot. You have to develop some parts of your character that were previously not needed and find a balance between being firm and loving. Here is a quick self-assessment that can help you know your strengths and help you to work on your gaps.

Can you be firm?
(1 = not very good at this; 5 = brilliant)
★ Can you say "No" to your child without feeling guilty or being worried they won't love you?
❐ 1 ❐ 2 ❐ 3 ❐ 4 ❐ 5
★ Can you deal with an angry, distressed child without feeling you might hurt them or want to hurt them?
❐ 1 ❐ 2 ❐ 3 ❐ 4 ❐ 5
★ Can you be very angry, but still be in control of what you say and do?
❐ 1 ❐ 2 ❐ 3 ❐ 4 ❐ 5
Total up your firmness score out of a maximum of 15.

Can you be gentle?
(1 = not very good at this; 5 = brilliant)
★ Are you comfortable cuddling, kissing or holding your child?
❐ 1 ❐ 2 ❐ 3 ❐ 4 ❐ 5
★ Is it easy for you to tell them you love them and what you appreciate about them?
❐ 1 ❐ 2 ❐ 3 ❐ 4 ❐ 5
★ Do you like to spend time playing with them?
❐ 1 ❐ 2 ❐ 3 ❐ 4 ❐ 5
Total up your gentleness score out of a maximum of 15.

Please don't use this test to make yourself feel bad, but to target where you can start to develop more. Everyone finds it hard to discipline a toddler, and we all learn as we go.

Some of us have to work at being more loving and warm, taking more time to enjoy our children. Others of us need to learn the skills of firmness while keeping a good sense of humour.

tears. Something else is needed to satisfy this little determined person who hasn't yet got much language or reasoning ability, but does know what they want...

2 Redirecting – the positive way to guide toddlers

This is the most commonly used strategy for early toddlerhood. Because your child doesn't have much language ability yet, the best method is to redirect them, not away from, as in distraction, but parallel to, their desires. For example, your child is at the kitchen cupboard, screaming, arms outstretched and looking at the biscuit tin. If you don't want them to have a biscuit right now, then maybe you can think of some other food they *can* have – a piece of carrot, a cracker and peanut butter, some cheese. Something to keep them satisfied without filling them with sugar or spoiling their appetite for lunch.

By doing this you are saying, "I understand you are hungry, I can help you with that (but I'm not giving you the particular food you asked for)." As they learn more language, and learn how to wait a little longer, you will be able to put a biscuit on the table near their lunch plate, which they can have when they've eaten their lunch. They will be learning that while they might not get exactly what they want, their needs will be considered and something good will happen. But they might just have to wait a little while! Quite important lessons for the whole of life.

When children have only the beginnings of language, it doesn't work to lecture or scold. And explaining everything in detail might be good for their language development, but not very effective in making them change. Two- and three-year-olds learn with their bodies, so showing them with actions is better than just talking on its own. For example, if they are pulling your hair, you make a noise; "Ow! That hurts me." You look at them and show pain on your face. But then (and this is the magic part) take their hand in yours and softly stroke your hair with it. As you do this, you say, "Gentle." Smile at them, and tell them, "I like it when you pat my hair gently." They get to feel in their muscles and skin, and see with their eyes, the results of getting it right with another person. You can also use this method to teach them how to pat a dog or stroke a baby sensitively. They will love getting the positive reaction that this brings.

As they become better with words, you can use redirection by putting all your words into the positive. Tell

children what to do, as opposed to what not to do. For instance, "Hold onto the side of the boat" rather than "Don't fall in." "Put your foot onto each step" rather than "Don't jump down the steps, you'll trip." This simple but profound change is one of the secrets of a happy life. Not only children but also partners, friends, employees, in fact everyone you deal with, responds better to being told *what you want, rather than what you don't want.* Try it and see!

It's easy to crush a child with a loud voice or threats – but at what cost? If you find your three-year-old and his friends having great fun bouncing on the new couch in their shoes, you could shout at them and make them ashamed (or rebellious). Or you could offer the alternative of the trampoline outside or an old mattress, or just ask them to take their shoes off. So instead of feeling bad or naughty for having fun, they learn that it's okay to have fun, as long as you think about where to have it. Even when there is no easy alternative, you can still stop children without making them feel bad about it. "I'm sorry to stop you having a good time. We have to look after the new couch. Let's look for another game that would be fun." It takes a little while to learn to think this way. You may feel like screaming hysterically on finding your toddler stirring the water in the toilet bowl with your best mixing spoon. But providing a plastic bowl, clean water and some old utensils in the kitchen or garden might be a better solution.

Activity and exploration is a sign of toddler health and intelligence. Remember they are doing what they are supposed to – and your job is to channel all this energy and intelligence into good directions.

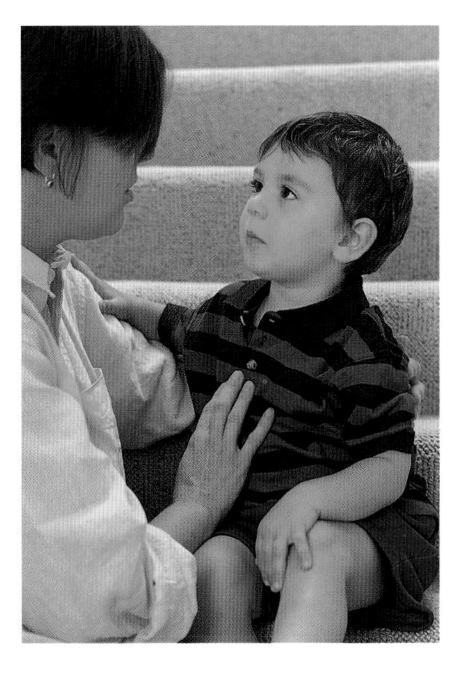

Discipline is all about helping them work out what to do.

3 The teaching conversation – the heart of discipline

Of course, it isn't long before redirecting is not enough either. From the toddler years until they start school, children's thinking skills and physical skills are developing in leaps and bounds! There soon comes a time when they know exactly what they want, and refuse to let the matter drop! And sometimes the answer simply has to be "No". We need a way to help them learn how to drop something that just isn't going to work for them, and be able to think and change their own behaviour – in other words, self-discipline.

As a baby, if they cried we'd come running to help. If they cried louder we'd come twice as fast. But now they are older, we are expecting to see them develop some self-control. We want them to:

- ★ learn to wait
- ★ take no for an answer
- ★ ask politely for what they want
- ★ respect others' feelings
- ★ not hurt others, with hands or with words
- ★ follow simple rules.

They are now big enough, strong enough and quick enough to get into all sorts of trouble and harm themselves in dozens of ways – turning on hot taps, running into the road, playing with electricity. So they need to learn certain rules in order to keep safe.

It doesn't work to just preach to children about these things. You have to teach them in hundreds of practical situations. No-one else can do this as well as you, because you love them and have the detailed knowledge of them. Discipline takes time. Often you can do this "on the run" – just conversationally helping them to work out what to do. But when children dig in, or are repeating the same problem over and over, which all toddlers do, then you can use the process described here.

The "teaching conversation" is a simple method you can use to help a toddler learn to do the right thing. It's a discipline method that helps children to find new ways to behave that still meet their needs, so that eventually the problem doesn't recur. Here's how it works: when a problem behaviour has happened, stop the action, calm your child if need be, and make good eye contact. You may want to have a chosen place in the living room or kitchen that you take them to for this conversation. You might tell them to come there with you, or carry them there, and hold them there with you if necessary. Sit or kneel down with them and wait until they are ready to talk. In a matter of fact voice, talk to your child and ask:

1 ***"What happened? What did you do?"***

"I was playing with the soccer ball and knocked the lamp over."

2 *"What were you thinking and feeling?"*
"I was just having fun."
3 *"What do you think you should have done differently?"*
"Played outside with the soccer ball."
4 *"What will you do to fix this now?"*
(This will have to be negotiated. The child might offer to help pick the lamp up, apologize, make a promise about future ball use – whatever you can agree to being a good outcome.)
5 *So will you do that now?*
"Yes."

This is abbreviated and you might have quite a bit of discussing and clarifying at each stage. Also your child might not be so good with words and need a bit of help. Adjust your expectations to their ability. The aim is that you feel resolved and that your child has taken in the lesson, but has come out feeling okay.

To do "the teaching conversation", you have to have time and be feeling reasonably calm. If you are "stressed to the max", then just use time-out, diversion or any technique that works in the short term. The "teaching conversation" is especially useful when you want to get to the bottom of a recurring problem and sort it out. You might find yourself using it a number of times a day for a little while (you can use it anywhere), then less often as your child grows older. The aim is for your child to exert

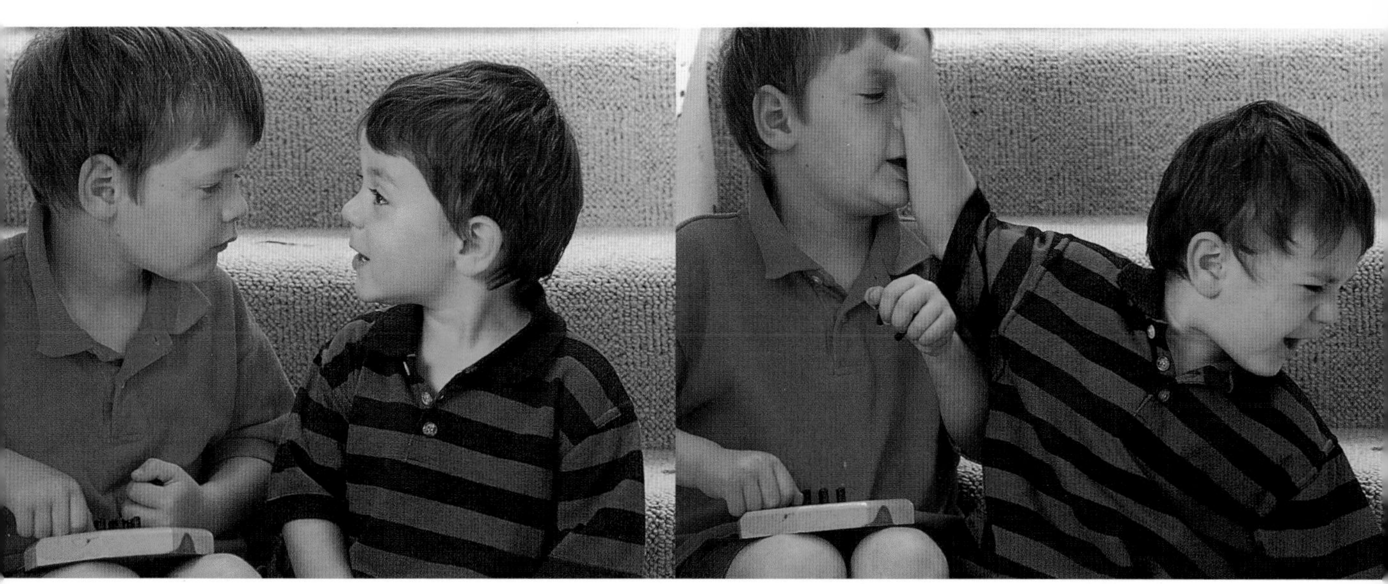

self discipline in future so that problems do not recur. Your child is not being punished, although as they grow older natural consequences can be included. They don't have to feel bad. But they are quite definitely being asked to develop thinking skills to figure out what happened, and their part in it. To consider their feelings and wants, and the feelings and wants of others. And to take responsibility for their actions. They come away with a plan of what to do now and something to remember in future that guides them to better ways. The result should be that everyone feels better afterwards.

A child has to be old enough for you to use this method. This means that they must first:

★ have some language skills
★ be able to understand and use words like, "Sorry", or "I did it"
★ make cause-and-effect connections like, "I pushed the table and the flowers fell on the floor."

Creatively avoiding conflict

Parents get very creative with ways to avoid head-on conflicts with toddlers...

Jacqui offers them a (limited) choice: "Because my son likes to have a say in what happens, I worked out this neat trick – I let him choose between two acceptable alternatives. I say, 'What would you like to wear today – your boots or your trainers?' This way he doesn't hassle about putting on his shoes; he feels like he's in charge."

Corinne hides a few toys away: "My kids have so many toys, but still get bored and don't know what to play with. I put a lot of toys away in a cupboard and bring them out like 'new' from time to time. I keep some toys aside to take on trips so I can get them out on the bus or in a waiting room, and they will be fresh and interesting."

Dave always keeps a few food and drink supplies on hand: "I noticed two thirds of all our conflicts were over food – usually the kids demanding sweets or snacks in shops. Now I carry interesting snacks and drinks from home and feed the kids when I notice them getting a bit hungry or bad tempered. I always keep dried apricots and a big bottle of water in the car."

Good things to try

Feelings, faces and animals

This is a very valuable activity, yet it needs no planning – just some time when you are together and the opportunity occurs.

In it, you use facial expressions to teach your child about different feelings.

- "**This is a sad face.** See, my mouth is drooping. My head is leaning forward. My eyes are looking down. I might sniff or cry. Can you do a sad face?"
- "**This is an angry face.** My eyebrows are pushed together and down. I'm staring hard with my eyes. My teeth are tight. My lips are pushed together. Can you make an angry face?"
- "**Now I'm scared.** I'm biting my bottom lip. My forehead is crinkled. My eyes look about quickly. My shoulders are hunched up. Can you make a scared face?"
- "**This is a happy face.** My mouth is smiling. My skin is soft. I might even be laughing. Now you show me happy; sad; angry; scared. Now you guess which one I'm showing you."
- **Benefits:** This speeds up the process whereby children learn to read, in a person's face and behaviour, what that person might be feeling. It leads on to helping them to know the most useful ways to act around a person who is having strong feelings. It encourages children to be sensitive and helps them to be good with people. Finally, and perhaps most importantly, it helps them to understand and express their feelings.

Learning feelings from pets

Pets have many benefits for children. The (slightly idealistic) idea of learning responsibility through caring for a pet is well known. But little children need help to learn to read the body language of animals they meet. It's especially helpful to show a child the signs which tell when a cat or dog is unhappy (that is, losing patience). When a cat flicks her tail, puts her ears down or starts to miaow, she might be angry and could scratch or bite. When you go near the dog's food, and he starts to growl and flattens his ears, that might mean he is warning you to stay back. It is his food and he is protecting it.Your child will be able to identify with this. An explanation will result in the child being confident and careful around animals.

At the same time, they will avoid unhappy encounters through bad timing. Very young children can be taught to pat and stroke animals gently, instead of grabbing or pulling. Show them and hold their hand to demonstrate. They will see the dog wag its tail or the cat purr. Tell them, "See, you have made him happy."

Teaching with sensitivity

Always remember to consider your child's feelings too. Perhaps today they are tired and having trouble coping. Ask yourself, "Is what I expect too hard for them at this age?" We have heard parents complain about children not using good table manners – at age two!

It gets easier

You will find yourself using the "teaching conversation" quite often to begin with. Sometimes it will just be casual and conversational, at other times it will involve going to the thinking and talking spot, and going right through the process before allowing them to move on. The result should be that when it's over, you should both feel settled and happy with no hard feelings. If not, then perhaps you have missed a step – perhaps you haven't got to the bottom of their feelings or found a realistic plan for them to follow to replace the old behaviour.

Gradually two things will happen: your child will co-operate more easily. "Please would you go and bring in the toys from the garden," will be all that is needed. And also, they will be clearer and more verbal: "Mum I am angry that you didn't keep your promise." This will keep you on your toes.

A firm but loving attitude is the key

You are helping your child to understand their feelings, figure out their wants and needs, and be effective in finding friendly and good ways to meet those needs. Discipline isn't for a parent's convenience or for the sake of peace – though that certainly helps. The aim always is to give your child increasing self-management skills and self-awareness: "I am sad that my friend is going home. I know I shouldn't have hit his mother's leg for making him go! I'll say sorry and please could he visit again soon?" It's possible by the end of the toddler years to have a beautifully people-skilled child. A child who behaves well (for a four-year-old), knows what they want, and can express their feelings clearly. Their spirit is like a bright flame because they have rarely encountered fear or humiliation, yet they are self-possessed and thoughtful too.

A Father's Diary

'Rudeness concert'

The invitation, casually delivered, was to a Concert of Rudeness. This appeared to possess possibilites, like a childhood Theatre of the Absurd. As the promoter was also the director and principal performer, I followed her to the venue the bedroom she shares with her younger sister. "Say a rude word," commanded the director. "Bum!" came the shouted reply. "Say another rude word," said the director. "Bugger"! The show was going well, the temperature of offence rising. "Say another one!" "Thumb!" I could see the director pause. "Thumb, thumb, thumb!" chanted her young assistant.

There was a puzzled look on the director's face. She had primed the gun of umbrage, aimed it at the adult world, and now saw it rapid-firing harmlessly and unexpectedly away from the target. Of this, however, her young assistant was supremely unaware. All she knew was that she had, quite literally, provided the show-stopper. "Thumb, thumb, thumb!" she was shouting, her freckled face beaming with malicious delight. It was a sort of perverse innocence.

As the audience of two filed from the bedroom, I again noted the director, leaning against her bed, face abstract with thought. Something had been lost in the performance.

Good things to try

A restful environment and a quiet time

People respond to atmosphere. For example, the noisy, harsh atmosphere and bright lights of the supermarket can make us hurried and tense, whereas in a quiet candlelit restaurant we can wind down and relax. You can create an atmosphere in your home to calm down your child and yourself. If you are sick of loud noises, agitation, busyness, be sure to do something about it. To encourage restfulness and softness:

★ *cut down stimuli* – turn the television and radio off; play gentle music or none at all; close the curtains; light candles, if you wish (careful of any fire risk here)
★ *have a soothing drink*
★ *give your child calming drinks,* such as warm milk, or cool chamomile tea
★ *have a slow bath together* – after the bath, spend some time holding, talking gently or singing, with your child wrapped in a warm dressing gown. Read a story.

Quiet time for older children

Once, most human beings lived in villages and on farms, and the atmosphere was quiet, reflective, with plenty of time for solitude and exposure to nature. When it was dark, people slept. Music and sound were made naturally or there was quiet. As parents, we certainly appreciate this idea, but children need it too (although they may not realize it). Explain to your child that this is their quiet time. The length can vary from 2–15 minutes, depending on the age of the child. Explain that it is something important to do that they will soon start to enjoy. They are not to play, talk or walk around. Your child can sit somewhere pleasant – on a bed looking out to the garden, on a couch by the window, on a chair in a sunny spot. Help them to experience the different sensations in their environment – for example, ask them what they can feel when touching pillows, a chair, clothes? What can they smell? Or taste in their mouth? Can they hear any sounds, like birds, the wind, traffic, breathing? What sensations can they feel on the inside of their body? Have them look at their surroundings, then pick something to study in detail. They can then close their eyes and imagine seeing inside their body, hearing, tasting and smelling, inside as well as outside. The first few times, take the child through all of these steps and soon they will be able to do them without help. This can be done routinely once or twice a day, or if the child needs to be settled down during a busy day. It becomes a lifelong skill which is useful sometimes when they are upset for some reason, such as starting school, visiting the dentist or dealing with teasing.

Kids and jobs

The first "job" of children is to have fun and, luckily, most are highly qualified! Four-year-old Brendan's mother told us, "He just loves to play. He will play with anything. Give him two rocks and a stick and he is in heaven!"

Happiness grows naturally. When a baby is loved and cared for they will take pleasure in simply being. As they grow and become physically capable, they will also automatically learn the pleasure of doing.

Kids start their learning by copying the things you do for them. A six-month-old baby will try to feed you their soggy toast! (You will look pleased and pretend to eat it while trying not to gag!) A toddler will bring you a "tup of tea" (a toy cup filled with sand). They will pick up things you dropped, "Here yar Mum." Soon they demand to help and to be self-reliant, "Me do it by self." They will put their wellies on back to front, and defiantly try to walk in them rather than seek help. They will squeal if you try to speed up their buttoning. They also copy older children, trying to be just like the big kids. It is natural for children to learn by imitation. Let them copy you and work alongside you whenever the chance presents itself.

At first we can help our children to do things for themselves. From holding their own cups, to eating, dressing, toileting and so on. Then they will start to learn to do things for others.

To begin with, teach them simple things like being gentle when they play, picking up things, being polite, saying "thank you" and "please", "hello" and "goodbye".

As they grow, the tasks can be more advanced – like making a bed, or helping to make their own lunch for nursery.

We all learn to work, and along with it we learn a cheery or grumpy disposition towards that work. It's in the toddler years that this attitude gets established.

Good things to try

The mother turtle game

This is a warm-hearted game, symbolic of healthy growing up, from a secure beginning.

Like all games which involve getting down on the carpet or lawn with your child, it brings closeness and fun for everyone.

★ ***Help your child to roll*** into a small ball on the ground. They are now a turtle egg. The mother turtle (you) covers the child's body with hers and folds her arms around the front of the child's head, being careful not to "break the egg". She then tells a short story – that she is a big, strong and proud mother turtle, who has laid her special egg in the warm sand.

★ ***With her hands flattened*** out, she pretends to scoop warm sand up and over the turtle egg to keep it safe and warm. She says, "Nobody can touch my egg" and slaps the surrounding ground to protect the egg. "But wait a minute," she says, "What is that? A little wriggle?" Then there are lots of wriggles coming from the egg. "It must be ready to hatch. Yes!" Out comes a beautiful, shiny, new turtle who is off to play in the sand and swim in the sea. When sharks or big fish come, it swims straight back. It can go to sleep in the nest, then head off again.

★ ***Benefits:*** Children really love this sort of activity. They enjoy the sense of protection and enclosure, then they love the feeling of breaking through and being welcomed out of the egg. It seems most useful from the age of about two-and-a-half or three, when many children struggle with the ideas of whether they are a big girl or a little girl, a big boy or a little boy. They may ask to do this activity a lot at a certain age, then lose interest or return to it later. One five-year-old literally grew out of it when he asked to try it again and found his body wouldn't fit any more! Make up your own characters – lion and cub, penguin and chick, kangaroo and joey!

"When we were kids in the 40's, times were tough, and my parents had to really work hard with six children and not much money to go around. We always worked together, and had good fun and laughed a lot as we worked, even though it was quite hard. To this day, I enjoy being active and doing things with other people." ***Doris, 58***

Rewarding your child's efforts

Here are some guidelines:

★ keep jobs simple and rewarding – two-year-olds can pick up their toys and pack them away before bed

A bathtime conversation ...

This tape was made a few years ago, by language specialist Peter Downes, of a conversation with his two-year-old son: Chris. Chris, went on to get a first-class degree in Modern Languages – which just goes to show the value of friendly chatting while you give a bath or change a nappy!

P: *Can you hear the water going down the plug? It says glugluglug, doesn't it ? Listen... glugluglug... it's all gone now. All the waters gone. The bath's empty, all gone.*
C: All gone.
P: *Yes, it's all gone, look.*
C: See my boats!
P: *What's that?*
C: Boats.
P: *Your boats?*
C: Des.
P: *They've gone now. We can't sail the boats in the bath, it's empty.*
C: (starts to cry) Boats!
P: *We'll do your boats another day.*
C: (crying again) Boats!
P: *They're not here, your boats love, I can't see your boats anywhere.*
C: Trapes, trapes.
P: *Trapes?*
C: Shtrapes.
P: *Tapes?*
C: Des, boats and shapes, boats and shapes, boats, boats and shapes.
P: *I don't know, I can't tell what you're saying. Are you having a little joke?*
C: Des.
P: *I thought you were.*
C: Ah.
P: *First of all let's put your nappy on. Shall we do that?*
C: No.
P: *Yes, there it is, nice clean nappy – make you comfortable for the night. There, there we are. One pin, one pin in that side, that's one pin, and now another pin in this side. Is that right, Chris?*
C: Des.
P: *Good. Now then, something else, we need ... plastic pants. There we are.*
C: Book.
P: *Yes, that's a book. We'll read that book when you're dressed shall we?*

★ show enthusiasm and praise them at first: "That's a good job"; "I really like what you've done"; and "Doesn't the floor look nice?"; "All the toys are safe in the box now."

Eventually all you'll need to say is, "Okay, it's bedtime, so tidy up", comfortably expecting the job will be done and simply accepting that it has been.

You give praise at first so your child feels good about their accomplishments. But don't overdo it. Eventually they will gain satisfaction just from being competent, and contributing to everyone's well being.

Good things to try

Making a special play space

Kids like to have a spot of their own – a seat, room, desk, cubby hole or whatever. Sometimes deliberately creating a separate space can help children to concentrate on an activity, or make them feel special and powerful. It doesn't have to be big, expensive or separately built.

★ ***Boxes*** Collect boxes from supermarkets – they create fabulous castles, forts, shops, shelves, cars, targets for bowling or goals for throwing a ball into to increase ball skills. If you get one big box (from appliance shops), all the smaller ones can be stored in it.

★ ***Couch*** Pull the couch out a little, creating a special cubby space between couch and wall. It's a good place to spy on Mum from and the jumble of toys can stay there out of sight.

★ ***The "nest"*** This is wonderful for children who want to be part of the action all of the time. They may not want their daily sleep anymore, and become tired and grumpy – not wanting to rest but at the same time not able to stay up. Look out for a big, open, low basket or cut down a large cardboard box, into which you can place pillows, sheepskins or soft blankets to make a "nest". This is the resting place, where a warm bottle may be consumed at leisure, while listening to taped music or a story. Little children love to snuggle in a nest; it becomes associated in their mind with "quiet time".

★ ***Knock to enter*** Bedrooms matter a lot to children. At times, you may notice that your child wants a little more privacy. Perhaps they want to be treated as an individual or they just get a fright when people burst into their room. Experiment with knocking first and asking, "Can I come in?" It's surprising how children feel more respected by this simple courtesy.

You will know this in your own experience – it's nice to be praised, and there is also the inner satisfaction of knowing what to do (fixing a flat tyre on a lonely country road for instance – you're just glad you can do it!). It's okay to say things like, "We all help each other in this family"; "We all like living in a clean and tidy house".

Our young children liked the movie *Mary Poppins*. (This film is full of messages about lovingly taking care of children, and at the same time helping them to be tidy and helpful.) You will hear the song that says, 'For every job that must be done there is an element of fun'. Children can (and often spontaneously do) sing songs as they work. Another fun working song from *Snow White* is 'Hi Ho, Hi Ho, It's Off to Work We Go!' At our house we often put on rock-and-roll music when we are working. Then we "get down" and "clean up"!

Giving your child specific jobs to do will help to raise his self-esteem.

Good jobs for kids

Here are some examples of first jobs (from two years of age):

★ put away toys at bedtime
★ empty a small wastepaper bin
★ take their plate to the sink after a meal
★ hang up the towel after a bath
★ put dirty clothes in the basket
★ tip water into the dog's bowl
★ use a dustpan and brush to sweep up.

You can choose any of these tasks or others that are more suitable for your child. You will have to explain the job, show them how to do it the first time, help do it with them if needed, supervise, encourage them and remind them, and still keep it light and pleasant. You will soon see that this is not aimed at making life easy for the parent in the short term. Teaching kids takes energy, but it's a real way to build self-esteem, which praise and adulation alone can never do. Self-esteem comes, eventually, from competence – knowing you can do things well.

During this toddler time you will be discovering that you no longer have a needy baby, but an emerging person who is often great company.

SHELTERING THEIR INNOCENCE

PROTECTING CHILDREN FROM SEXUAL ABUSE

It's up to us to do our very best to keep our children's bodies, hearts and minds safe from sexual abuse.* Early, inappropriate exposure to sexuality can cause fears, distress or mysterious problems, which parents can be at a loss to understand. So what can we do?

A child's first line of protection is the quality of everything we do with them as parents. We don't expose them to danger, are careful who we entrust them to, we always listen to their feelings and concerns, and we teach them to value themselves. To this general quality of caring we can then add specific steps, including those to the right, which were suggested by experienced parents...

** Sexual abuse occurs when an older or more knowledgeable child or adult uses a child for sexual purposes. It can happen to any child, even a baby, and the abuser may be a man, woman, family member, trusted friend or opportunistic stranger.*

1 USE THE REAL WORDS
Teach children the proper names for body parts – vagina, vulva, penis, nipples, anus and so on. This gives them more ability to talk about their body and takes away needless mystery.

2 TALK THE LANGUAGE OF FEELINGS
Help children to identify and be able to express what they are feeling – happy, sad, scared, unhappy, angry, and so on. They will be better able to talk to you about their feelings when they do have a concern.

3 USE RESPECTFUL DISCIPLINE METHODS
which do not involve fear. If you don't use hitting as a punishment, or physical or verbal threats, and you listen to their side in a dispute, your children will always know that they can come to you, even if they feel guilty, and you will listen and not hurt them.

4 TEACH THEM THE "STOP!" RULE
In games you play with them and they play with each other, have a rule that anyone can say 'Stop!' and this will be respected. Ensure that all players obey that rule. This is very important in letting children know they can call a halt to anything they are uncomfortable with. (This is also useful for adults who are arguing.) Part two of this rule is that, if they say 'stop!' and the other person does not comply, they must move away and get help from someone older, if necessary.

5 Teach and value privacy

Gradually introduce the idea of privacy. Point out that adults don't undress or touch their genitals in public, and explain that you want them to follow these conventions too. If someone doesn't stick to these conventions, your children will know something is not right.

6 Don't sexualize your children

Dress children age-appropriately – it's best that they don't dress as miniature adults. Don't joke about young children having "girlfriends" and "boyfriends".

It can be disturbing for young children to witness sex, either in reality or on television or in films.

7 Abolish secrets

Don't use or have secrets as part of your family life. Children should not be expected to keep things to themselves. Children who are told or threatened by someone that they must "keep a secret" will know this is wrong and that their parents expect them to tell. (Use the term "surprise" if you are talking about a birthday gift or party.)

8 Be careful about sleepovers

Children should only stay the night at someone else's house where you know all of the family well and when it is clear that no other visitors will be sleeping-over. Have an understanding with your child that they can phone you at any time, and you will come and get them. You could have a code phrase – like, "I'm feeling sick" – in case they are too embarrassed to discuss it with or in front of the carer.

9 Trust your intuition

Act on your feelings. Often, the only warning of child abuse is an intuition you have about a person or situation, that "something isn't right". Even if you have no facts to support you, it's okay to say no to an invitation or situation you don't feel 100 per cent comfortable about.

10 Don't push your children to be intimate

Encourage them to kiss or hug only those people you would kiss or hug, and then only if they want to.

11 Go with them into public toilets

We need better and more single-entry toilets, or parent-child toilets, in public places.

12 Respect children's bodies

From about the time children are out of nappies (three to four years), no one but themselves should specifically touch their genitals, unless for a medical examination. They can learn to wash and care for their own penis or vulva and, if they have a problem, it is best if they show you, and for them to do the touching, rather than you.

13 Be careful with carers

Have very high standards about who cares for your children. Make a practice of dropping in unannounced from time to time, even (especially) when this is discouraged.

the special job of father

chapter 6

What's a man to do?

> *"The ghosts of his entire ancestry spring up on the beach beside him, offering things to say..."*

It's a sunny spring day and he is at the beach with his small daughter, exploring the rockpools. She is searching blissfully for crabs in the crevices, chatting to them and rearranging their social lives.

Without noticing, she has moved further and further under a cave-like overhang. Then suddenly she stands up and hits her head very hard on a ledge above her – sharp needles of rock impacting with her skull. She wails, then tries not to wail, then wails some more – a scream almost – as the pain intensifies.

He feels a swirl of responses. The ghosts of his entire ancestry spring up on the beach beside him, offering things to say... "You silly girl, why weren't you more careful?" "Come on now, it's not that bad. Stop making that racket." "Oh, it's my fault, I should have watched out for you better." He manages not to say any of these things, sends these ghosts packing. Instead he scoops his daughter into an enveloping hug and, after a moment, gives her head a rub to numb the pain a little. She seems comforted, and calms down, sobbing just a little in his arms.

As they walk back homewards, her hand slips into his. He feels good, grateful to have got it right, for once. Her hand in his says, "Thank you." His hand says, "Yes there is pain in the world, but I will be here for you."

Becoming a confident dad takes time

If you are a confident father from the moment your first child is born, then there's something wrong with you! It's true that we men often feel that we are supposed to "have it all together", "know all the answers" and "be ready for anything". To be kind of an SAS-man-supercool-high-tech-genius-father. Well, I have news for you – it isn't like that.

Fatherhood is something you slowly get the knack of. It comes to you from hanging around your children as they grow up through all the ages and stages. You start out clueless, you make all kinds of mistakes, and then one day you realize you just got through a whole day with the kids without any real dramas. Everyone is fed, in bed, warm, safe and with all their fingers and toes intact. Like any

kind of newly acquired competence, it's a good feeling. One day, when you see a younger dad, unshaven and red-eyed, struggling with a baby plus a toddler in the high street, you can grin at him sympathetically, and think "You'll get there mate!"

There are naturally some obstacles to arriving at this happy state. Your own childhood is probably the biggest of these. If your father lost his temper a lot, or never played with you, then you might have to consciously shake off these limitations, and not make them yours too. In a heated moment you might find yourself yelling just the kind of stupid things your parents yelled at you when you were small.

> *"One day you realize you just got through a whole day with the kids without any real dramas."*

Another danger is complacency – you get really used to your child being a four-year-old, and then all of a sudden they're eight! This continual stretching of your fatherly capacities is all how nature planned it, so don't worry – just stay humble and keep learning.

There are only two things to remember:

* you are truly important in the lives of your children
* you are human and so are your kids, so don't be too hard on any of you.

The difference fathers make

We live in sad times. From watching television or reading the papers, you could get the feeling that fathers don't matter. Women have babies through sperm donors, millions of single mothers do their best to raise children around the world. But fathers do matter. The body of research is vast and very clear in its conclusions that having a caring and involved father in the home improves children's chances in every aspect of their future lives. For example, doing well at school, staying out of trouble with the law, having a positive self image, getting a job, avoiding violence or teenage pregnancy; all these improve out of sight if you have a dad.

Not every dad gets it right though, and no father is consistently good at it all the time. Being a father is hard because it's a balancing act between extremes. You have to help make a living, but not let your work swallow you up, leaving no time for your kids. You have to be able to

> *"Being a father... is a balancing act between extremes."*

share the discipline, but not get too mean or become just the family policeman ("Wait till your father gets home!"). You have to listen to your partner's point of view, but also be true to what your own heart is telling you. You steer between extremes by making little corrections as you go along – just like the way you steer a car. "Hang on my voice is getting a bit loud." "Everyone's getting tired and cranky, maybe we need to stop for a drink and some food".

Most fathers around the world do a pretty good job, and they always have. You would not be here today if not for the courage, competence, commitment and love of thousands and thousands of fathers through the ages. So genetically speaking, you've probably got what it takes!

Good for girls, good for boys

Throughout history men have been active in raising children, teaching them and playing with them. Only in the industrial era did we get the crazy idea that women raise children and men just work to pay the bills.

Now this is changing. In fact, more than ever before, dads and mums today are interchangeable. We've realized that either sex can be a great parent. In many families today you will often hear the little children mistakenly call Dad "Mum" and vice versa. This is something that would never have happened in a 30s' family, for instance. In some of those old-style families, it was like the room went cold when "Father" walked in. If your kids confuse the two of you, congratulate yourself. You are in equal standing, as the big people they can count on from long experience. Your love and availability is like the water they swim in every day.

In spite of the skills being interchangeable, there is a unique way that women do things, and a unique way that men do things in the family. Everything a man does, he does as a man. He isn't "getting in touch with his feminine side" when he is nurturing children or fixing dinner – that's a very sexist idea. When a man hugs a baby, he's being masculine. Everything he does helps his children get an idea of maleness. If he is good to his partner, and also self-respecting if he is good with

children, and capable in the big world; if he is happy with his life, that's a powerful message to his son and his daughter.

Finding a gender identity

The thing is a boy knows he will become a man, and so is interested in how a man behaves. Even two-year-old boys seem to naturally imitate their dads, and will often challenge them to get a reaction. If a dad spends time with a son, accepts the child's feelings, and also shows his own feelings, then the boy will become emotionally healthy and look forward to being a man.

If a girl finds her father to be trustworthy, and safe to be around, and enjoys his company, then she will have a good start in relating to the opposite sex. This can be very important in years to come. One study found that teenage girls with involved fathers waited on average 18 months longer before becoming sexually active, which has to be a good investment! Researchers believe girls with caring fathers set a higher value on themselves, and are less inclined to have sex just to get the affection of a boy. Because their dad treats them well, they expect at least this level of respect from boys.

It's important that fathers communicate respect for a girl's ability and intelligence, and never behave in a sexual way towards their daughters. At the same time, they can

be respectful and still be warm and close to their daughters; in fact this seems to be important in raising a girl's self-esteem.

There are two genders in the world, so it helps if there are two genders in the family too. (Gay couples, as well as single parents I have spoken to are usually very aware of this and take steps to make sure they introduce opposite sex role models in their families. A role model is not just a person passing through; it means someone who is present in the child's life for enough time that the child can imitate them in many different situations.)

While the under sixes are only just beginning this road to gender identity, it is so much better if children feel the love of both parents right from birth. This way they can get a good start along the road to relating comfortably to both genders as adults.

The great thing is that finding a gender identity is a natural process for children. We should not impose any of the old rubbish about girls being cute and helpless, or boys being macho and unfeeling. We can actually treat boys and girls pretty much the same, and they will find their own way to be the person they are. Your daughter may well enjoy wrestling games, and exploring the outdoors, and your son may enjoy making food or helping in the kitchen. They will be 21st-century multi-skilled children, and yet still be confident of which gender they are, because they have experienced maleness and femaleness fully in their parents, and their parents' friends, and can choose freely their own identity.

Why dads stir kids up

It's too limiting to say this is what dads should do and this is what mums should do. Every family must make the best use of the natural strengths and talents of both parents. But some general patterns emerge in cultures worldwide. You don't have to hang around with families for long – at the park or at the beach – to notice that fathers often play with children in a much more boisterous and physical way than mothers do. They disrupt, energize and activate children. (This can be a bit of a nuisance at bedtime, when mothers are just trying to calm them down!)

Research has shown that children with involved and playful fathers seem to react better to stress and change, perhaps because dad's playful roughhousing (rolling on the floor, pretend wrestling, acting out wild animals) has accustomed them to enjoying a bit of adrenaline. Rough play isn't just for fun; you also learn things from it. Boys learn an important lesson from this kind of play – they learn how to be excited and yet not hurt themselves or

how children melt our hearts...

"the story of Livvy the mouse"

Our house is in a forest. The forest bursts with life, and much of it determined to make its way to our kitchen or bedrooms. From time to time, hungry bush rats gnaw their way into the pantry and we have to lay poison to get rid of them.

So one morning, up early, my daughter of five years and I stumble down to the kitchen, and she is running on ahead of me, so there's no time for a "cover up". Ahead of us, in full view on the clean white lino, making no effort to escape, is the tiniest mouse, looking very ill. My daughter, always the nature girl, hushes me authoritatively, peers at it closely, and before I can protest, scoops it up gently in her hands. Its all I can do to stop her from giving it "mouth-to-mouse" resuscitation.

I say something like, "Oh, I think it's poisoned. It's probably going to die" – thinking that by getting this out straight away, I can somehow save her some distress. But she is determined it will get well. With me feeling very mixed emotions, we organize a cardboard box, some water and food, a bit of grass for a nest, and she is persuaded to put the trembling ball of fluff in there.

She immediately gives it a name – "Livvy" – the opposite of "Die-ey", I guess.

I am dimly aware of feeling cross with her, perhaps to keep at bay my own helpless feelings about the grief it will surely cause her. It does cross my mind too, that with her sharp five-year-old mind she will soon figure out who is to blame for laying the poison.

I try to calm myself down, to accept the fact of how she is feeling. I put an arm around her as we peer into the box. I say, "I think it will die, honey. It's eaten some of the rat poison; it can't get better." She starts to cry. She folds into my arms, and we both let the sadness come. She is crying at first for the mouse, but almost straight away something very interesting starts to happen. The little rivulet of her grief suddenly opens out into a deep river. "It's not fair," she sobs. "Everything is dying. The dolphins and the trees". She is almost wailing.

"They don't look after nature. It's all dying." You can feel the downward swoop of this most ancient of griefs. Now I am cursing all those "Save the Rainforest" cartoons and the stuff they learn at school. We burden kids with this stuff, instead of doing something about it. Yet it's more honest than pretending things are fine.

After a while she stops sobbing, and seems more than just over the pain, somehow to be more deeply at peace. I am struck by the miracle that the mouse has triggered a deeper grief she has been carrying, and has released an unexpressed pain around her little heart. A pain that was already there, and which could have cramped and harmed her body and spirit.

I am suddenly grateful for the mouse, and pleased that I was able to just be with her in this precious moment. She of course is undaunted now. "The mouse will be fine she says. Livvy will be fine."

A postscript: later that day, we came back from the shops to find that the corner of the cardboard box had been chewed through to a mouse-sized hole. Livvy was gone – he had revived, it seems, and had made his escape. Life holds on. I wish him and his family all the best.

others. Good fathers seem to naturally monitor the safety of the play, sometimes stopping to say, "Hang on, we need some rules," or "You can wrestle, but don't hit" or "Careful of the furniture!" By having an adult involved in the rough and tumble, rather than it just being between kids, then some maturity and care can be learned. In this way, boys who have an explosive kind of energy can learn to moderate it, channel it and be responsible while still having fun.

Fathers are often (though not always) the outdoor specialists. They especially seem to like taking the children out and exhausting them! They often encourage kids to try harder and be braver. (Dads also have more accidents with children, so you have to watch out and monitor risk-taking.) With little babies, it's often the dad who takes them on his shoulder and walks the highways and byways, giving the mother a much-needed break. Kids all over the world have adventures with their dads – they learn to see the world as exciting, they get exercise and co-ordination, and sleep better when they come home.

Pregnancy and birth – the big transition

You might think it's the woman who goes through all the changes of pregnancy, but actually men go through a lot as well. Many of these changes are very positive. You will probably feel lots of tenderness and protectiveness towards your partner, some excitement, even some awe – there's something sacred about a woman's ability to bring about this miracle of baby-making.

There are negative feelings too. Many men freak out a little during pregnancy, which is very natural given such a big change. You might notice some insecurity, as well as feelings of "Am I ready for this?" Nobody ever is! It's natural to wonder, "Can I handle the responsibility?" but remember that parenthood is *one day at a time*. You will certainly get anxious if you start worrying about which university to send them to.

If you have bad feelings that last more than a day or two, then the best thing to do is talk – don't just keep these feelings to yourself. Talk to your partner, and also talk to male friends who are further down the path of raising children, about what it's like and explain how you are feeling. They have the perspective of time and will (hopefully) help you get a handle on it all.

Sex and pregnancy

Your partner's interest in sex might swing around wildly during pregnancy – from none at all, to highly motivated. If you have come to think that sex is like beer in the fridge for you to just go and grab when you feel like it, then you might be in trouble here. This is a growing-up time. Real, mature men make love with their partner by invitation, kindness, care and respect. If her hormones are changing, or her body is uncomfortable, then respect her feelings. At the same time, don't give up if you want to win her affections. Patient and sensitive pursuit builds attraction. Talk about the timing and what she needs to relax – you could massage her or cook the evening meal so that she can save some time and energy for you. Some men go away and sulk, or act grumpy and impatient. Surprisingly, most women don't find this endearing or seductive! There might be other ways you can satisfy each other, than just regular intercourse (outercourse, for instance!).

A pregnant woman still wants to be reminded that she is a woman, a lover and a partner, even though she is somewhat preoccupied with physical challenges that having a baby bring. Many men find their wives deliciously beautiful at this stage, and many women are delighted and amazed to hear this, because they can feel quite the opposite – cumbersome and unattractive. "Feeling like a beached whale" is the usual complaint.

Part of the challenge of pregnancy for a man or a woman is the need to be a little separate from each other as you get ready

for your new role. Don't be panicked by this – you will have a deeper relationship as a result of it. This is the time to find your own feet emotionally. Take long walks while you can, read books you have wanted to read for a while. Build up a sense of emotional self-sufficiency, even though as a couple you are very close.

You have seven or eight months to prepare, so don't waste it. You can learn massage, cooking, cleaning, nappy-folding in advance! You can practise living to a budget, healthy eating, and quit smoking and using drugs.

Don't get into crazy last-minute house renovating if you can possibly avoid it. You have to be able to calm and nurture yourself, instead of looking to your partner as the source of all your wellbeing. It's parenthood, and the maturity which it requires of you, that helps to make you a man. Standing on your own feet actually means you are more adult, more able to be close (as opposed to being clinging), more able to give and take as the need arises.

As birth approaches

It's natural for many of us to feel scared for our partner as the time of the birth gets close. Part of this is that you feel protective, and yet can't do a great deal. In the antenatal classes, and at the birth itself, you may feel you are at best a helpful supporter. But just being there is exactly what is required of you. Look for a birth place that clearly welcomes fathers and includes them in the birth process – whether it is homebirth, a birth-centre birth, a hospital room, an operating theatre, or in a caesarean operation. Fathers should be able to be present and helpful in all these settings.

Sometimes our fears benefit from some exploration to find out where they are coming from and they can often be easily allayed by getting more information.

A personal story might help here to illustrate how deeply some fears can run, and where they can come from. During our first pregnancy, I found I was getting very panicky whenever the birth was discussed. I was puzzled by this, and one morning woke up having made the connection while I was sleeping. When I was three, my mother became pregnant with my sister-to-be. She developed some serious complications and we had to move to my grandmother's house so mum could rest. When she finally went to hospital to await the birth, I wasn't allowed to visit, so she sent me little toy figures with my father after each visit. Everyone was quite stressed and worried, until she finally returned home safely, with a new baby girl. Now, back in the present, my partner was pregnant, and part of my unconscious was mixing her up with my mother back then. I was irrationally fearful that she might die or disappear and never come back. It was very helpful to realize this and separate fact from fiction.

These days birth is very safe, especially for the mother. Fathers are not pushed out of the birth process like they were 20 years ago. (In our case, I insisted on being present at my partner's caesarean operation and was far too excited to faint. I took our son straight into my arms, and it was one of the best moments of my life.)

“Just being there is exactly what is required of you.”

We've got used to the idea that mothers need a support person before and during the birth. It might also be a good idea for there to be a male support person for the father. This ideally would be a man who has children of his own. He needn't be present in the birthing room, but available close by to bring food, encourage and talk to the father about how it's going, and help him to keep up his energy and focus.

A new baby in the house

This is the time when it all gets practical. Snatching sleep. Changing nappies. Accumulating dishes on the bedroom floor because you are just too tired to clean up. Your body in the first weeks adapts itself to getting less continuous sleep – after a while you won't notice. Take care crossing the road! Take a note of where you left your car. Turn off the gas. This is the time when parents-in-law miraculously change their image – becoming angels of mercy whom you embrace gratefully as they bring casseroles and offer to clean up the house.

Your relationship with your partner is suddenly very different, and this takes some getting used to. It's just possible that you will feel jealous that your baby has replaced you – that your partner is in love with an eight-pound Casanova. Talk to your partner often, and get her reassurance that you have her love and appreciation, if not much of her time.

The first year is tough, but gradually you get her back. Sometimes both of you will feel that you are more like shiftworkers than lovers. Be sure to devise some reminders that you still have a romantic view of your partner, even though she complains of feeling like a prize milk cow.

Don't, whatever you do, start calling each other "Mum" and "Dad". Take lots of photos or funny home videos. Ring up during the day to see how things are going, and don't panic if your partner is "fed up" – "How do you bloody expect me to be feeling?"

Don't be demanding. Some men we know have left their marriages because they couldn't handle the competition! At the same time, some women forget they have a husband, who matters too, as they fall head over heels into baby-bliss. (Some new mothers "hide" behind their baby, and comfort themself with a baby's love rather than deal with the demands and complexities of nurturing their marriage.) Both partners have to stay committed to feeding and caring for their relationship, so that it can thrive. So remind your partner pleasantly that you are still there and that you will give to her, while the baby will mostly just take.

Fighting to be a father

It's happening somewhere right this minute. A young father is taking his newborn baby into his arms for the very first time. He hasn't had much sleep for 36 hours, but you wouldn't know it right now – he's high on adrenaline and the dreams and hopes of being the best dad there ever was.

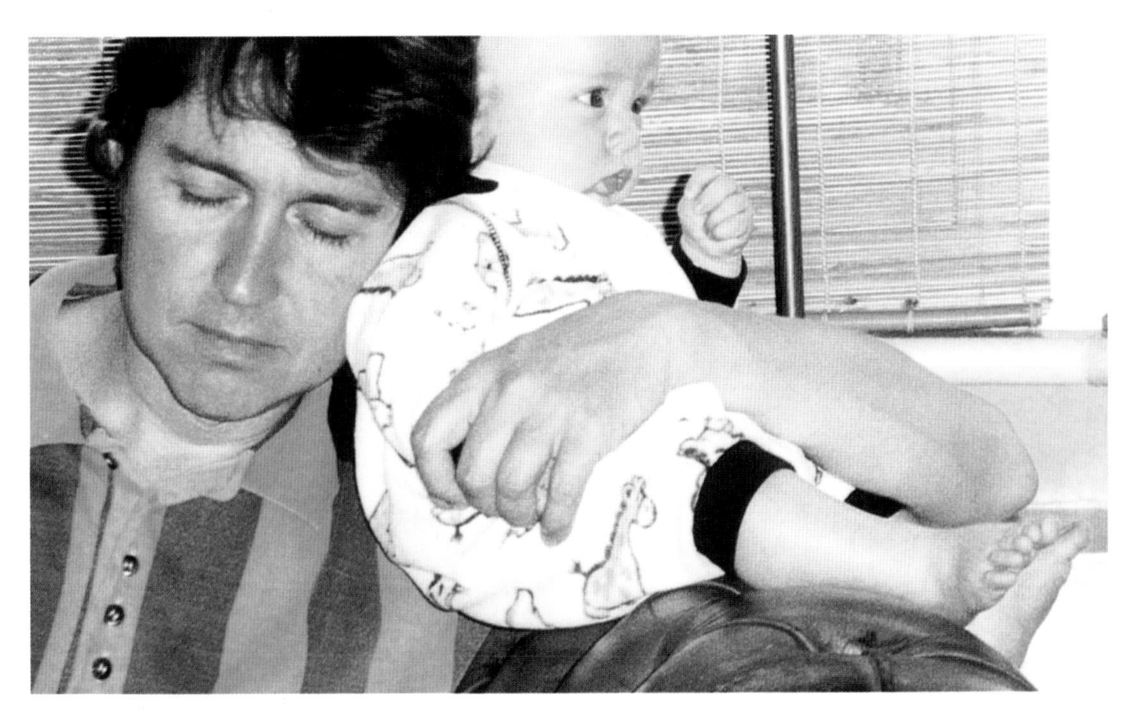

Men say the same things about being at the birth of their child: "It was unforgettable; the best moment of my life!" But watch them closely because, seconds after they say this, a shadow of sadness often passes across their face. For many fathers, especially in previous generations, it was all downhill from there. In the hospitals of the past, cool hands interceded, the baby was soon taken away, professionals took over. The father had his first taste of something he had to get used to – being marginalized and irrelevant.

The mother, with much more social support for her role as parent, would probably hold her own, and go on to forge strong connections with the child, but the father would increasingly take a background role. Being pushed aside was what 20th-century fatherhood seemed all about.

In the industrial era, being a good dad meant being a good provider – a walking wallet. He raised the money, she raised the kids. The ideal man of the 20th century was defined by what he didn't do – if he didn't beat his wife, didn't sleep around, didn't gamble or drink too much, then he was a good man. If he played the odd game of cricket with the kids, he was positively a saint. Nobody expected much more.

Our fathers' generation showed their love by working, because that was how society was organized. Millions of 20th-century men worked themselves into an early grave, at jobs they often hated. They were usually exhausted by the time they came home, and missed out on the close relationships and fun of family life. The stress and imbalance of this kind of life meant that the life expectancy of men – once on a par with that of women – was seven years less than that of women by the end of the century. The incredible thing is that fatherhood was not always like this. We tend to think of fathers in history in terms of the stern figures in our family photo albums. Yet researchers, such as Adrienne Burgess, have found that fathers in pre-industrial societies and throughout the hunter-gatherer era over hundreds of thousands of years were very active and involved in parenting. In non-industrial countries, even today, fathers are close to children, and spend hours a day teaching and caring for them.

Two hundred years ago, parenting manuals were aimed at fathers, and men were the ones blamed if children turned out badly. Centuries ago a third of homes were headed by single fathers (because mothers often died through poor conditions). A study of Civil War correspondence from soldiers found that details of children's lives were the central topic of concern. "Myself and the other men often talk about our young ones," one soldier wrote. And, of course, in the long pre-history of the human race, all men were teachers of the young, endlessly coaching and developing their kids, as if their survival depended on it – which it did. Now we are getting back to this healthy and healing pattern. Over five generations, the art of fathering was all but lost.

If you want to test this ask yourself, "How many of my male friends are really close to their own fathers ? And is this how I want it to be with my kids when they grow up?" The answer will be pretty clear.

Good things to try

I did it my way

Once your kids are about two years of age, or older, it's very good to prove to all involved that you, their father, can do the round-the-clock care – feeding, putting to bed, doing interesting stuff during the day, and keeping a house in some kind of order at the same time.

The best way to do this is a "women's weekend away" where your partner takes a hard-earned weekend away with her friends, and you look after your child or children single-handed. (This is assuming that you are not already the stay-at-home parent – if you are, then it's all reversed.)

The Women's-weekend-away project requires some planning. You could start small with just a morning at home, or a whole day. (Many fathers do this already, so this advice is more for the dad who has been working long hours while his partner did the babycare, and so hasn't done much "solo flying".) Perhaps spend a day while your partner is not there, but is available for help on the mobile phone!

If your partner has been the main carer, she can give you a detailed briefing. You will want to know:

★ *details of your children's routine* – when they like to sleep, and where, and with what combination of bears, bottles and blankets, storytelling or tooth-brushing rituals are necessary to induce sleep!

★ *what and when* they usually like to eat and drink

★ *safety concerns* – dangers they are currently likely to face, such as a pressing interest in the wiring of the stereo, or a loose gate latch onto the road, and general safety in the home. Perhaps they pull the dog's ears and may get bitten. You may not know that if you talk on the phone for more than 10 seconds, your children reliably go and eat unsavoury things in the garden.

This is all information that you will benefit from knowing – IN ADVANCE! This time you spend in total care of your children will be a wonderful initiation for you all. You will learn a lot (expect one or two big arguments or sort-outs to happen and the occasional, "I wish Mummy was here!"). The kids will know you much better at the end of it. (You might want to link up with some other fathers during the weekend for a trip to the park. Don't take them to your mother's – that's cheating.)

There's nothing like the quiet pride of knowing you can do it all. And anyhow, who cares about matching socks.

Rediscovering fatherhood

"Everywhere I travel I meet men who are determined to be better fathers."

Today, because of the two-hundred-year legacy of fathers being away at work, or war, young men want to be better dads, but often don't know how. This was certainly how it was for me personally. It is an odd experience, for someone who is supposed to be a parenting expert. Time and again, I strike a situation where I feel there is something wise or helpful I should do or say with my kids, but I don't know what it is! I know that there must be some pool of masculine wisdom that I am missing.

I watch how easily my partner Shaaron seems to know what to do, and learn from her. Sometimes I would do it differently, sometimes the same. I listen to other men with their children – sometimes gleaning good ideas, sometimes noticing they look as clueless as I feel. I think this is why so many of us retreat to the world of work. No-one likes to feel like an idiot. Everywhere I travel in the world I meet men determined to be better fathers, who are succeeding, often against all the odds, in doing so. I am convinced that this is a major social movement – a fathering renaissance that could change our world.

Sometimes it's just a matter of trusting your instincts. When I was holding my newborn son in the hospital while Shaaron was recovering, a nurse came up and wanted to put a foot-long stiff plastic pipe down his throat to get a sample of his stomach contents. I said, "Sorry sister, no way!" or something like that. I did my best to be polite, and to my surprise she said, "Oh, okay" and went away. A doctor friend later told me I had done the right thing – it was a pointless and traumatic procedure. All I knew was it sure didn't feel right to me! It was the first time all day that I felt really useful too; it quite cheered me up.

Things are going to get better and better for fathers as we win more family-friendly working hours, as we stick together to get better schools and hospitals. The men-with-women team has been kept out of parenthood for a couple of centuries, but it's a powerful combination of hearts, minds and hormones, and pretty much unstoppable when it gets going.

Special challenges

There are some classic pitfalls that probably every father that ever lived has had to negotiate. A daughter, even at the age of two, may notice that fathers like female appreciation. It's a small step from here to "She winds him round her little finger". Likewise, if a man is overly keen to be "friends" with his son, to the point that he can't risk upsetting him, his son will be very tempted to exploit this, and will end up spoiled.

"I love you Dad – can I have a pony?"

Being able to be firm with a child – boy or girl – is not difficult once you get started. While being generous and loving is fine, also being able to say, "No, no sweets today", or "It's time for you to go to bed now" or "You have to pick up your things" is essential for raising children.

Sometimes it's good to look beneath the obvious problem to the underlying causes. If you find you are so worried about your daughter's goodwill that you won't take a firm stand with her, then you may need to pay some more attention to your marriage. If you are looking to your son to be your best friend, you probably need more male friends.

There's another possible danger with boys. Some men feel they are in competition with their sons, and this can lead to harshness, being too aggressive, too loud, or unreasonable and mean. It can also come out through pushing them too hard in sport or school. Expecting they will be the next Boris Becker, and you will be their Dad! Watch out for this, and talk it through with your partner or friends, as it can do a lot of harm. We have to let our children be themselves.

Separated dads

It's very tough being separated from your kids. For a long time divorce courts assumed mothers would keep children, and fathers would have "access" to spend time with them. Gradually it's being recognized that both parents can play equal parts in raising children after divorce or separation.

Good things to try

Getting closer through play

Some men feel awkward with children and don't know how to play or talk with them.

Perhaps your own dad died when you were young, or wasn't around much, so you don't have memories of fun times and conversations between dads and kids.

Or it may just be that you haven't been around young children very much, and lack experience. The good news is that everyone feels awkward to start with. The way to overcome this is to just do it. As early as you can, get to know how to cuddle your baby or child, as well change nappies and get babies back to sleep. If you have never got on the floor and played with children before, just start.

Read them a story at bedtime. Don't worry about feeling stupid, that's just the point. Be stupid! Make funny voices. Pretend to be an elephant and let them ride on your back. Your children will feel so much more at ease with you and look forward to being with you and it will make trust and conversations work better when they are older, since they aren't afraid of you at a basic physical level.

If you are separated and so only see your kids part of the time, you need to learn to be balanced in your care of them. The biggest danger is that you will be a "Santa Claus dad", because you want them to like you and you haven't got much time. Resist the temptation to buy their affection with treats, and also the tendency to be tolerant of bad behaviour for fear of losing their affection. They will feel most secure, and that you care most, if you are firm with them. This means having consistent standards of behaviour and simple firm rules – like no hitting, no hurting each other verbally or physically, and so on.

Marriage breakup can be devastatingly sad for fathers, hard and very lonely, but it doesn't have to stay that way where your kids are concerned. Talk to other men, or find courses or organizations for separated and single dads. Your children will always need and want to know about you as their real father, even if your ex-spouse finds a new partner. Don't disappear from the scene, even though it is sometimes hard to stay in the picture. Get on with your life, and stay involved with your children's.

Most nursery schools and primary school classes have parents as reading volunteers, or other involvements, where you can be closer to their concerns. Get to know their friends and their friends' parents. Organize their friends to visit once trust is there, or share outings. Have your own relationship with their teacher, and monitor your child's school progress and how you can help promote this. Go to events at the school, and use a planner diary to keep track of these.

And of course, in as many direct ways as you can, co-parenting, as well as phoning and writing, sends a clear message that you want to be just as much their father. If you can work towards an equal-time, co-operative relationship with your ex-partner, and also have a steady and fulfilling life of your own, then your children will be comfortable and secure with you. This is a major achievement, but more and more men are finding a way to do it.

What if you are a single parent?

There is no point beating about the bush – being a single parent is hard. Single fathers find it hard to be both the father and the mother, giving tenderness and just managing the household needs, as well as making a living. Children give affection back to us, but the human design is for us to have an adult partner fueling our supplies of love. If you are a single parent, take care to keep up adult friendships, and have a life of your own. Don't let your children be your only support network. Don't use single parenthood as a safe retreat from the world. Find adult friends, and visit other people with children so they can socialize and play. Many single dads tell us they feel lonely and awkward at playgroups and nursery, with all those women around. Perhaps as more dads are doing the caregiving, this will change; we will see a lot more father-and-child groups and dad-friendly activities.

Fatherhood and your career

One danger of all this fathering stuff is that you can develop Superdad Syndrome. It happened to women, and it can happen to you too – the career success/super stud

/super Dad triangle that could give you a heart attack on the spot! It's time to become mellow and learn to accept moderation and balance in all your roles.

For instance, though kids cost money, they actually need your time more than your cheque book. If you have previously been a go-getter at work, it's not a bad idea to ease back a little when you have young children.

You will enjoy life, and have happier more successful kids, and a better love life, if you don't always grab that next promotion or work back until 8 o'clock at night trying to impress the boss. It's okay for your priorities to change with fatherhood.

Some of the changes in priority kind of sneak up on you. For instance, you go away for three days on a work trip. To begin with you are so pleased to be free again to sleep or stay up when you want to. But after two days, you find yourself in airports and shopping malls envying other people's babies, wondering if you'd get arrested if you gave a passing toddler a quick hug. Congratulations, you've joined the worldwide league of Dads. Men who have lost their competitive compulsions and don't care! Men who have slowed down, eased up, realized what matters and are in for the long haul! Even your view of women will change: "Wow, see how she handles that pram"; "Nice way with the pulverized vegetables!"

The common myth is that you will lose your business edge because of baby fatigue, but in fact you will become better on the interpersonal level – the emotional intelligence level. Good fathers make the best bosses, managers and team leaders. You will have more compassion, you will feel more interest and concern for your staff and workmates.

You may find you want to do work which improves the human situation, instead of just making a quick buck. You might even change jobs or move out of the rat race to a more satisfying line of work. Family life will give you depth and understanding of others which will make you good with people, and a deeper and better person all round.

Good things to try

Fatherhood essentials

Fatherhood is a bit like (I imagine) flying a plane. You try to cruise along, but keep trimming and adjusting, and occasionally wrestling the thing through a storm or two.

Below are some of the main "controls" you have to watch.

★ ***Make time.*** This is the big one. If you work a 55- or 60-hour week, it will be almost impossible to cut it as a dad. Fathers need to get home in time to play, laugh, teach and tickle their children. Sometimes fathers find that the answer is to live on a lower income and be around their families more of the time. Forget the television – go out to the park and play games. When you are together, make good use of mealtimes and bedtimes to find out about each other's day. These are significant opportunities for reconnecting and listening to their adventures.

★ ***Start early.*** Get involved in babycare – this is the key time for relationship building. Caring for a baby triggers your fathering hormones and changes your life priorities. Spend some of your days off giving around-the-clock care to your baby and child, so you know you can do it all.

★ ***Be warmer*** – hugging, holding and spending gentle time together telling stories or singing songs to them. Tell your kids how great they are. If you weren't given lots of affection as a child, now is the chance to learn.

★ ***Lighten up.*** Learn to enjoy your kids – being with them out of guilt or obligation is second-rate and quality time is a myth. Find the overlap – things you all enjoy to do. Take achievement pressure off your kids, but insist that they contribute in the home. Limit them to one or at most two sports or activities, so that you still have family time. Avoid competitiveness in any activity beyond what is good fun.

★ ***Heavy down.*** Some fathers today are lightweight "good-time" dads who leave all the hard stuff to their partners. Get involved in the decisions, supervise homework, kids' housework and discipline. Develop discipline that is calm but definite. Insist on respect, and make it mutual. Don't hit, though with young children you may have to gently hold and restrain from time to time! Don't just be one of the kids. Do listen to them and take their feelings into account.

★ ***Don't do it alone.*** You have to have help – other men, other women, who take part alongside where uncles and aunts used to be. Join a group of friends or a church or organization or sport that maximizes adults and children having a good time together, for its own sake, and honours and cares about the character development and celebration of children.

★ ***Be a proud dad.*** Be proud of your children, and of the part you play in their lives.

A Father's Diary

'Home from the party'

by Martin Flanagan

My wife is proceeding down the Princes Highway at 4.45 on a Thursday afternoon in the week before Christmas. The traffic, needless to say, is maddening. She is ferrying children home from a birthday party and each child is a pressurized organic container of hastily masticated icecream, hamburger, cordial and assorted confectioneries.

My wife is concerned for the boy sitting in the middle of the back seat, a small child with sleepy eyes. For the first six months of his acquaintanceship with my daughter, he mistook her for a boy and called her Richard. Their relationship has a gentle, dream-like quality. But in the half-hour before leaving the party, he has slowly acquired an unnatural pallor. In a lull in the traffic, my wife momentarily takes her eyes off the road, turns and inquires as to his wellbeing.

This innocent act signals the beginning of what I can only describe as an Amityville Horror for Under Sevens. A spray of regurgitated party fodder passes her nose with such velocity that it lands only marginally short of the dashboard of our trusty, rusty Subaru. It is as if a high-pressure hose has suddenly sprung a leak and is skidding about the car, spraying wildly and at random. The young girl on his left erupts like a mezzo soprano, leaping from silence to a high-pitched scream vocal bound. At this, the Birthday Girl, who is in the front seat and was buffeted by the original emission, comes out in sympathy and, between sobs, utters the historic line: "This is the worst day of my life!"

The Mezzo Soprano now adds a second dynamic to the drama. Shooting out a straight right, she pushes the head with the offending orifice as far away from herself as possible, with the effect that she stubs it like a cigarette into the lap of the third passenger in the back seat, another small boy. What alarms my wife, who is following developments through the rear vision mirror, is that the ill child does not return to the perpendicular but lies there, pallid and unmoving. Crises call for emergency measures. Taking a sharp left across the Princes Highway to the safety of the kerb, she delivers a sharp verbal smack to the two girls, now scaling operatic heights of passion and feeling in chorus, and establishes that the child has not expired but is merely sleeping.

And that is how I met them: one child asleep, two vibrating like motors, but doing so noiselessly, and the interior of the car looking as if a tin of pink salmon had exploded. And my wife, as is usual when things are at their worst, was laughing. I salute her.

chapter 7

the pre-school year

The age of looking outwards

It's a sunny day outside, and windy. Twenty-one mothers and twelve fathers sit in a good-natured group, looking forward to an afternoon of talking about parenting, sharing problems and solutions, and enjoying adult company and support.

They all share one thing in common – children in the age group 4–6. This is a challenging age group, because they are so dynamic and eager to learn – easily bored, hungry for social activity. It's also the age of the mind, and every child is a genius with a swirling, sparkling intelligence, hungrily swimming in the ocean of knowledge.

"Why do they always ask 'why' about everything? For instance,'Why is there air? Why is that lady so fat? Why do cows have legs?'"

Children of this age want things to do, places to go and people to play with. It's a time to visit other families so kids can play together. Adults also start to crave the company and the advice of other parents. Hence this seminar.

The group is comfortable together, and so we dive in the deep end and ask them, "What specifically do you want to ask about kids in the pre-school age?" Without hesitation, a torrent of questions starts to pour out...

- "Why do they always ask 'why' about everything? For instance, 'Why is there air? Why is that lady so fat? Why do cows have legs?'" "Yes!" exclaim a couple of other parents. "That sort of stuff. Does it ever stop?" "No!" joke a couple of others. There is good-natured groaning.
- One father, a bit of a joker, calls out, "So, how can you make children not speak for a year or two?!"
- "Why do they argue so much? They keep wanting to argue every little point. I thought I had them well trained and now they mutiny."
- "How can I keep them busy?"

- "How much television should they watch? And computer games – are they good or bad?"
- "My child is turning into a bully. What can I do about it? I yell at him and smack him and it doesn't seem to help."
- "Our boy is a real wimp, he always gets picked on. How can I get him to stand up for himself?"
- "I worry about my daughter being abducted. She is too trusting – should I teach her to be more afraid of people?"
- "Can I help my kids with learning to read?"
- "What can we do on long car trips?"
- "I hated school when I was a child. How can I prepare my children for starting school, so that they like it?"

So many questions. Our philosophy for these seminars is that parents know more than they think. Through discussion, and a chance to reflect, you can understand your children and how to help them. We add to this our own experience of talking with thousands of other parents, and what we can pass on that works. The best thing, though, is the feeling of parent power – sharing a common goal to be loving and creative towards our kids.

This chapter is based on the afternoon's highlights and the wisdom that the parents were able to discover together.

Dealing with children's questions

Sometimes questions have simple answers, and kids are happy with them. So, for "Why do cows have legs?" there's an easy answer, "Cows have legs to keep their bodies from rubbing on the ground." At other times, children are "on a roll", wanting to know more – so you can throw it back to them in a playful but helpful way:
"Why do you think?"
"To walk around? But why?"
"Well, what do cows like?"
"Grass!"
"So how do their legs help them?"
"To get to more grass!"

Sometimes questions can go round and round in circles, so decide if you want to talk or not. If you're busy, say so – don't get irritable or sarcastic. But remember your children are more open to learning at this age than later, and this is cheap education:

"Where does rain come from?"

"Where do you see it come from?"

"The sky, but how does it get there?"

"From clouds."

"Where do clouds come from?"

"The ocean. They blow over the land and drop the rain."

(You can try to outrun them too.)

"Where do you think the ocean gets its water from?"

(Long pause) "The rain!"

"Yep."

"Dad, do fish pee?"

Sometimes (often, in our case), you *just don't know* the answer. In this situation, discuss who your child could ask or how they could find the answer. Be genuine about it – go to the library together or look on the internet. Your child will be very impressed. When our children were little, there was a very good craftsman, called John Bright, who lived in our valley. Our young son always assumed John would know about anything technical. Other people were good to ask about nature and plants. His grandfather knew all about shells, and horses and sport.

At this age, children learn best by doing. Whenever you get the chance, don't just talk, but look, touch, feel, move, try out what you are talking about, whether it's showing your child a slug on the cabbages or explaining a piece of machinery you are putting together.

You might be busy, but if you can take time to enter your child's world of learning, then your pleasure will be multiplied. For instance, if they ask you about why a car's wheels are round, you can give them a ball or a pencil and show them how it rolls. Compare it with a wooden block, which won't roll. And so on. Steiner educators recommend not

Pre-schoolers have wonderfully open hearts and minds.

imposing your explanations of the world, but helping the child to arrive at their own at this age. They believe too much theory can get in the way of the child's direct experience.

Some questions kids ask are far from trivial. They might suddenly ask you about death, for instance, because they have just realized that their grandma is old and that old people die. It's worth taking a while to talk this over. A seemingly small question might lead into very deep water if you have the time to go into it. The Russians have a word for "soul talk", which means having a long conversation while walking in the countryside or sitting by a stream, where life's big questions slowly come out and a child's real concerns can be talked through.

Again, it helps to be concrete and practical. For instance, if you have a respectful ritual for burying your child's dead goldfish, then they may be better equipped and more able to handle the possibility of a death of someone they care about.

Separating truth from fantasy

At this time, when fantasy and imagination are blossoming, many and varied are the pretend friends and imaginary adventures that children will create. One day they are showing us "Cat Land" or "Snail City" and we are enthusing with them. But next day, when they tell us the snails took the chocolate cake from the fridge, we have to draw the line! The first time your child lies to you, it can come as a shock. It's a normal stage, so don't panic, but help them to make a distinction in their own mind about what is real and what is made up. A young mother in the group offered this example: "We were at a playgroup picnic and there was a donation box that Shelley was sitting near. I never gave it any thought. On the way home, I saw her playing with a line of small coins, so I asked her, "Where did you get them from?" and straightaway she answered, "From your purse." I knew my purse was empty, and so I had to make her tell the truth. It was very upsetting."

Sometimes it's hard in new situations for children to weigh up right and wrong, as temptations (or

Good things to try

Stimulating the imagination

There are dozens of little games you can play to entertain and pass the time with a child.

★ *Hand games* Hold up your pointer finger and have a pretend lasso in the other hand. Make the action of lassoing the finger, then pull on the end of the pretend rope and make your finger bend accordingly. Pull it up, down, over your head, around your neck, under the table, and so on. Now hand the end of the pretend rope to your child and let them tug it gently, or say it has come undone and you have to tie it on again.

★ *Stories* You or your child start up a story and take turns in adding to it.

Child: "Once there was a witch."
Parent: "And her name was?"
Child: "Vera was the witch."
Parent: "And she had two pockets in her britches."
Child: "She had itching powder in one and a frog in the other."

In another story starter, you use the name of the child and their best friend, for example: "One day, Lewis and Rohan were going for a walk and they came across a box left in the middle of the road..." Ask the child to make up the next sentence. When they stop, you add another, and so on.

Or you can set the story in familiar surroundings, for example: "One Sunday morning, Dad went outside and saw our old blue pram rocking and shaking, and when he went to look in it he saw...'

Make the stories ridiculous, hilarious, scary, surprising or problem-solving – the aim is to have fun together.

★ *Thinking games* This is a pretend game to stimulate your child's thinking skills and imagination. It can be played anywhere.

Parent: "Let's play the pretend present game. I've got a present for you." (Parent thinks of something exciting to pretend they have to give the child.)
Child: "Okay, thank you."
Parent: "Now you have to guess what it is. It is big."
Child: "Is it a horse?"
Parent: "No, it's very big and round and blue and wet."
Child: "A swimming pool!"
Parent: "Yes!"

opportunities!) occur. With their new-found powers of explanation, carefully developed by you, they realize they can fabricate explanations after the fact. Don't let them confuse you. Help them to think back to what was happening, and what they were thinking and feeling at the time.

After helping her to be specific, and to remember what happened, Shelley's mother told her, "I understand what you are saying – that you wanted the money. I know you like saving up, and it looked like anyone could have it. But you felt it was wrong to take it, because then you pretended it came out of my purse. That's true isn't it? (Pause) Do you know who it does belong to? (Pause) Now what can you do to sort it out?"

Shelley went with her Mum to give back the money and apologize. The chances are good that Shelley won't make up "tales" another time – this was fairly uncomfortable for her. It's important to note that her mother was gentle enough that Shelley could admit what she had done, and didn't feel blamed or bad, just mistaken. She will learn from this that it's possible to get back to the truth, and sort everything out.

Sometimes it's hard in new situations for children to weigh up right and wrong.

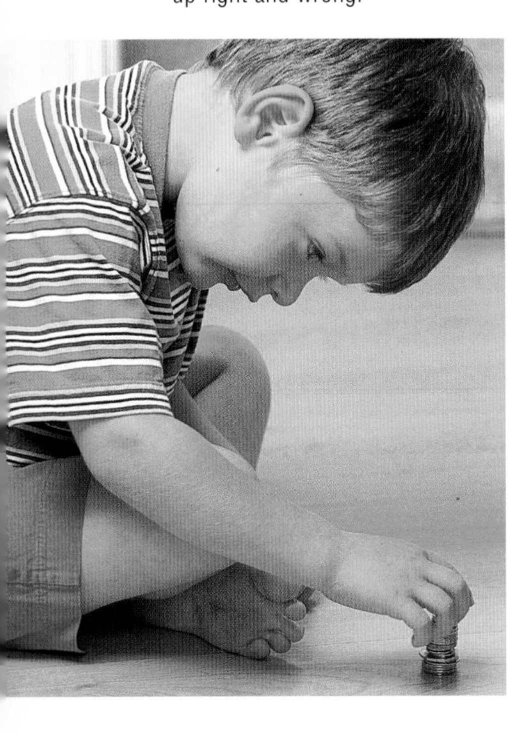

Staying honest

Keep reminding children of the truth as you encounter different situations. For example:
"I'm as old as Phillip."
"Phillip is 10 years old, you're 4 years old!"
"You said I could have an icecream today."
"No I didn't."
"Well, Dad said I could."
"Okay, let's check that out with Dad."
(or, "So if we go and ask Dad, what will he say?")

Honesty is a two-way street. We must be honest in our dealings, because children will pick up on the dishonesty, and even "drop you right in it!". Here's an amusing instance we heard of.

A tired Mum had just got her two toddlers and a baby to lie down for a rest, and was horrified to see the approach of Mrs. Maloney up the path to her house. She just didn't want to talk to this long-winded but kindly old neighbour today. So she whispered to the oldest child who was still awake, "Shhh, just be quiet and go to sleep." When Mrs. Maloney returned later that day, the four-year-old bounced up to her and announced, "We hid from you before!"

Everyone has stories like these. One child we heard of was being introduced to his new class. Asked to tell the class where he was from, he said, "London." And what work does your father do? (A risky question at the best of times.) "Oh, he's into drugs."

A four-year-old asked his grandma at Sunday lunch, "Is your neck better now Gran?", "Why?" asked the old lady, looking confused, as the parents stiffened visibly around the table. "Well," exclaimed the child, "Dad said this morning you had a pain in the neck... or something like that."

Repairing mistakes

Mistakes are an important part of life. If you can't admit to mistakes, you have to pretend you're perfect, which is very hard work. Or you have to never try anything new, which is limiting.

One of the greatest gifts you can give your kids is the sense that it's okay to make mistakes, as long as they also try to fix them. This may include:

- ★ apologizing – being willing to admit we were wrong, and say sorry
- ★ openness – explaining our intentions, and "where we are coming from"
- ★ telling the truth – and owning up to our actions (as mentioned earlier, this means separating reality from wishful thinking!)
- ★ taking responsibility – fixing the damage and paying the cost.

You might find you have to help your child to apologize to someone from time to time – to give back a toy they brought home for instance. Stand by your kids at this age as they fix their mistakes, to make sure they neither get unduly persecuted or rescued. You are aiming for a relieved feeling to be the outcome. If you are unsure what kind of reception you and your child will get, privately ring up first and explain what you want to do. Other parents will understand and most shopkeepers will welcome the apology.

Sometimes kids persist in stealing or other unacceptable behaviour as a cry for help when they are having other problems, or when they are feeling neglected. They should still sort out the problem as explained earlier, but we need to be alert to what may be the underlying cause. An important question to ask yourself is, "What was going on in the child's life when this problem first began?"

A final point – kids only really learn the skills that we have mastered ourselves. So we need to demonstrate this behaviour in our dealings with them. When we break an agreement or forget a commitment, we should say sorry, fix the problem and not use lame excuses.

Kids keep us honest. We can show them how mistakes can be turned into positive outcomes. The result will be real poise and maturity for us and our children.

Janine walked into her five-year-old son's bedroom to find him quickly pushing a chocolate wrapper under his bed. "He looked so suspicious," she told us. "I knew something was amiss!" It soon became clear he had taken the chocolate while they had been at the shops earlier that afternoon.

"Richard, I'm really upset about this. Those chocolates belonged to the people in the shop. You shouldn't take them without paying."

"Mmm..."

"What can you do to fix it?"

"I won't take anything ever again."

"That's good. But what about this chocolate bar?"
"I can't take it back, I've eaten nearly it all!"
"So what do you think you can do?"
"I don't know."
"Well, you took it without paying for it. They cost about 50p. I think you need to go back to the shop and explain, and give them 50p from your money box."
Richard went very pale!
"Can you give them the money Mum?"
"No, I didn't take the chocolate. You need to fix this with the shopkeeper. I'll come with you."
"Oh...okay."
"How about we go now?"
"NOW!?"
"Yep. You'll feel much better when it's fixed."
As they drove to the shopping centre, Janine asked Richard to figure out what he would say to the shopkeeper.
"How about saying I accidentally took it?"
"No. That's not true. What is true?"
"I took it without paying, and I'm sorry I did. I want to pay for it now."
Janine also felt a lot better when this was over. Luckily, the shopkeeper was amused and very co-operative – though he behaved sternly enough for Richard to get the message.

Good things to try

Jobs...

Possible jobs for three- to four-year-olds include:

- ★ ***setting the table*** – ask your child to count how many people, place mats, pieces of cutlery are required, and to place them correctly on the table.
- ★ ***after the evening meal,*** scraping scraps into the bin; putting their own plate and cutlery on the bench; wiping place mats with a cloth and putting them in the cupboard, drying up the non-breakables.
- ★ ***replacing the toilet rolls***
- ★ ***feeding the cat or dog*** with food from a cup (later learning to open the can as well).
- ★ ***putting toys away before bedtime.***

Sometimes parents designate a particular day of the week – usually Saturday or Sunday – as their children's regular jobs day. Others give each child one job per day, plus daily self-help chores including:

- ★ ***taking off pyjamas*** and putting them in the right place
- ★ ***getting dressed,*** doing up buttons and zips
- ★ ***hair and tooth-brushing.***

These are general ideas only, and need to be varied with your child's age and capabilities. Each child is different, and there are no comparisons. You will be sensitive to your child's own timing. When they are ready to try something new, there should be no pressure or need to hurry them. They don't have to grow up too fast.

Four- to five-year-olds

By the age of about four-to-five years, it's good for your child to learn about money. Some parents start to give pocket money for doing their regular jobs for the family. Others give it as a right. You might try a combination and find out how you and your child feel about it. A basic wage, plus bonuses! Young children don't need, and shouldn't have, a lot of money to spend. They need to develop a sense of value which comes partly from shortages! However, a small amount of pocket money is an interest, and encourages counting, figuring out what they most want, waiting, and saving, and understanding why parents go to work!

Doing the dishes

Four-year-olds can learn to dry dishes. Use a chair seat as a low working surface for them. Put a towel on the seat. They can work here with less risk of dropping things. Start them with saucepans, spoons, plastic utensils, bowls and so on, working up to flat plates which can be placed on the towel-covered seat, wiped, turned over and wiped again.

What if they don't want to do it?

Sometimes children will go on strike. One day it's, "Let me help Mummy" and then the next day, "No, I won't do it!" By the age of three they are getting to know their changing feelings. They are also starting to test out, "who's in charge around here?" Now is a good time to begin giving explanations as to why we do things the way we do.

They can understand simple reasons, such as, "If you leave the toys there, they might get walked on and broken." "Nana asked us to come to her house tomorrow, so we have to do our jobs today." "If you put your bowl up on the table, the dog won't get it (again!)."

You can also use a little humour – offer them a grimy cup for their drink, and they will figure out for themselves why we do washing up.

Remember jobs you choose for this age group should never be backbreaking, frustratingly difficult, totally inconvenient, or excruciatingly painful to perform, even though they may try to convince you that's exactly what they are! Remember you've specially chosen tasks that are simple and no big deal, and that's the way you want your child to treat them. This is the time for learning to follow reasonable instructions, without hassling, feeling bad, arguing or whingeing. Don't let them work with precious, expensive or breakable objects. They don't have the necessary co-ordination yet. Stay close by and engage them by showing them little extra ways or short cuts. Always, when teaching children jobs, try to do it in a spirit of enjoyment and co-operation.

Be sensitive to when your child might have difficulties and be willing to be flexible in what you expect.

Getting the job done

Teaching children about "getting the job done" raises all kinds of important lessons, for instance:

- ★ trust
- ★ responsibility
- ★ remembering
- ★ being prompt
- ★ caring about others as well as yourself.

By talking these over with your smart pre-schooler, they will begin to understand these values as they are getting older and ready for school.

A Father's Diary

'The veil'

by Martin Flanagan

She bought the veil for 75p at a fair. It had an elastic strap and flowers embroidered above one ear and, that night, when we went to the Pizza Hut for tea, she insisted on wearing it. The next day, when I took them to the park, she put it on her doll, Penny, who was in her pusher. A two-year-old boy named Joey, who was being pursued around the park by a woman dressed in black saying, "No Joey, no", borrowed the pusher and headed off in the direction of Port Phillip Bay. By the time Joey was apprehended, the veil had wrapped itself around one wheel, been severely stretched, and had two holes torn in it. This did not perturb her. The next morning, when it came to go to kindergarten, she emerged from her room again wearing the veil. "What will the other kids say?" I asked warily. "They'll say, 'It's beautiful, can I have a go?'" she replied.

We had to pick up her best friend who travels with her each day to kindergarten. The friend came bounding up to the car, pulled open the door, and announced, "Look at the new dress I'm wearing." On the other side of the seat, as demure as a bride on her wedding day, sat my little Madonna waiting to be noticed. There was a pause, and then the friend, in a voice shrill with truth, said, "You look stupid."

If it had happened on the steps of the altar, or at the door of the registry office, I could not have felt more for her. I saw her illusions punctured, but that evening, when I got home, she was again wearing the veil. I asked her about the interaction with the friend. "Oh," she said, philosophically, "She says things like that."

Helping your child to change habits

We all love our children, but sometimes we may not like them! Bad habits like whingeing, fighting their brothers and sisters, shouting or leaving stuff about and being thoughtless, are all hard to live with. For your sake and for theirs, so that they can become good to be around, it is worth making an effort to help them.

Firstly, have a think about whether their behaviour is just a sign of their individuality coming through and whether your annoyance is really *your* problem. For instance, creative, talkative, musical, inquisitive, and lively kids can be a trial, but we don't want to squash their vitality – just turn it down a little.

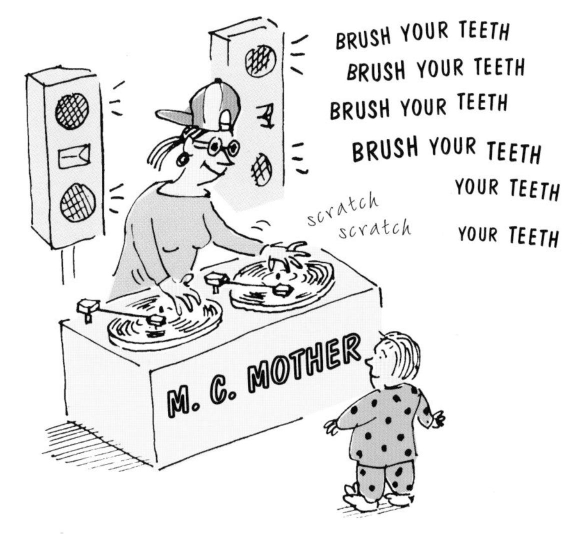

Often though, a particular habit will clearly be a problem for everyone around and bring bad consequences for the child, which you can foresee and they cannot. This is where we need to remember that we can dislike a behaviour, but that doesn't mean we dislike the child.

What's behind the behaviour?

Children can't always see what is going wrong for them, and often need our help to get out of patterns they are stuck in. For instance, they probably won't come to you and say, "How can I make more friends?" It is more likely they will say, "Nobody wants to play with me" or, if they are even less mature, they may just go around hitting or fighting with other children.

We have to help them pinpoint what is going wrong, and rather than just pushing our solutions, such as, "You

must work hard at school" or "You should be good at sport", we need to find out what kind of help they really need. In the case of a child who has a problem with hitting other children, the help they need might be skills in making friends. You can help them to learn to join in games with others. Or perhaps they need practise at speaking in a loud, strong voice when they are angry, instead of hitting people. The only way to find out which goal is the right one, is through talking to them. You can find out if they are really lonely at nursery, say, or just angry because of a child who always takes their toys. You can ask them or their teacher, or just watch for yourself.

A sequence for learning new ways

Here is the sequence which you can use to track down and overcome a pattern that is holding your child back. You will find in the years from three to six that you are often teaching and helping your kids to negotiate the world of other people. Effective parents don't leave this to chance, nor do they blame their child – but say, "Okay, how do I teach them to get it right?"

Here is a simple way to do this:

1 **Choose your goal.** You already know what you *don't* want your child to do. The first step is to turn this around and specify what you *do* want:

★ for whingeing... use a normal voice
★ for not obeying... do it straightaway
★ for hitting... use words to let people know you're angry
★ for being a loner ... join in the game.

Sometimes there might be a problem which you have with your child, which they are blind to. A child may not see it as a problem that they ignore you when you ask them to do something. But they would agree with you that the big fights and yelling that result would be worth changing. So you can point out how changing this would benefit them too.

2 **Consider possible reasons for the behaviour.** Begin by asking the child for their reasons. They may or may not know. Also think over any changes or circumstances that could have triggered the problem. Often children's behaviour is their way of showing upset over something – their Dad's illness or everyone fussing over their new baby sister. Perhaps what you are asking is unrealistic for their age. Perhaps there is a physical cause you haven't yet discovered – co-ordination trouble, eye problems, allergies, or hearing impairment, for example. These are worth investigating.

3 **Decide to act.** Once you have eliminated underlying causes, and feel comfortable that this is a

straightforward new lesson that your child needs, you can get started. Explain to your child the new plan, what will be happening from now on, and the goal you are aiming for. For example, if they tend to hit other children when a dispute arises, you explain, "It's okay to be angry sometimes, but when you are angry you have to use words, not hands." Explain that they are not allowed to hit other children. Instead, in a conflict, they should ask politely first, and if that doesn't work, use a stronger voice. If that doesn't work, then they should come and get your help to sort it out (or a teacher if it's at school.) Expect that this will take some practise. You can even make a game of it, so they can practise using their "strong voice" on you.

For a child who does not join in well, teach them good ways to join in. They could:

★ say "Hello, my name is______, what's yours?"
★ ask to join in a game that is already going on, "Can I play too please?"
★ look for someone who is on their own and ask to play with them
★ take a toy or game to share. And so on.

You might invite children they like to come and visit so they have more chance to build up a friendship. It will take a bit of experimenting and encouragement to get right. Most children have a bit of trouble with friendship skills to begin with, but soon overcome any difficulties.

The method is the same whatever the problem – figure out what new behaviour your child needs to get over the hurdle they have struck. Break it down into bite-size skills, then teach them how to achieve it. It takes a bit of thought and time, but is so much better than just blaming them or giving up. The last points in this list are some extras that will help to reinforce what you are doing:

4 **Look at yourself as an example to your child.** Sometimes we have to fix the problem in ourselves first. If we solve problems by hitting our child, then we can hardly expect them not to hit too. If we don't go out and make friends, we can't expect them to be good at socializing either.

5 **Be positive.** Notice every little improvement they make, and encourage them by pointing these out and congratulating them. Keep imagining your child as having already achieved the goal. Say encouraging things like:

★ "I know you are good at playing with other kids. Go and ask if you can join in."
★ "You are very clever at working things out. Go and try again."
★ "You got the first part right – you picked up your toys and took them to your room. Now you have to think about the right place to put them."

The parents in our afternoon group had lots of examples. We got in and worked on a couple of specific ones which you may identify with.

Dealing with whingeing

Jane, who had astonished the group by having four children under eight years of age, and still being able to smile and speak coherently, started with a question about her six-year-old.

"I've got one that whinges. She really gets me down."

"What do you want instead?"

"I want her to not do it!"
"Not talk? Or not whinge?"
(Jane laughed).
"Would you like it if she used a normal voice?"
"Yes!"
"Why do you think she whinges?"
"Well, I'm pretty busy with the baby. She just goes on and on at me, until I give in for the sake of peace."
"So it works!"
"Yes, I guess it does."
"Smart kid."
"But annoying! I can't stand to be around her. It gets me down!"

There are two reasons for whingeing that we encounter all the time. One is – it's the only "wavelength" that gets through. If the child asks normally, people don't listen. This is common in big or very busy families. Secondly, the parents themselves use whingeing voices, and the child is speaking the family language! The group was amazed how well Jane coped with all these children. Whingeing was a relatively small problem in the circumstances. Jane and each of her children were so much in need of individual time together, and more relaxation. To get started on the immediate problem though, Jane was happy to consider the following steps.

How to help your child speak pleasantly

1 **Demonstrate** what a normal voice sounds like, and then how your child's usual voice sounds.

2 **Practise together** a whingeing voice and a normal voice, saying the same words. Make a game of it if you like: (It's really pretty funny!) "I'm hungry Mum!"

3 **Tell them** you will only listen and help them if they use a normal voice. This doesn't mean they will automatically get what they ask for even in a normal voice – just that they have a better chance! You can explain, "You asked for that really well. But you can't have a biscuit because tea is almost ready."

4 **Notice** the next time they use a pleasant, normal voice, and tell them you've noticed.

5 **Remember** not to answer questions and not give them what they want unless they are asking in a normal voice. Occasional reminders will keep them on track. The interesting thing you may find is that a child's whole personality can change once they change voices. How you sound affects how you feel. If you speak more evenly you feel better, and if you don't sound like a "victim" you won't be one. This is a profound and important change of attitude to life.

Dealing with bedwetting

Margaret looked like she'd been waiting on the edge of her seat for this chance. "What about bedwetting?" "Yes" added her husband, Harry.

Their five-year-old son, Jason, was still wetting his bed. It was annoying, smelly and worrying, since their other two kids stopped by the time they were three. Margaret and Harry were really "peed off"!

"So what is your goal?"
"No more bedwetting."
"Put it in the positive. What do you want?"
"Dry beds."
"Good. What do you think might be behind his behaviour?"
"I think he's just slack. He can't be bothered going to the toilet" (this from Harry).
"Could be. How about you, Margaret, do you agree?"
"I don't know if he is lazy – it upsets him too. He cries about it sometimes."

We went on to give some background. The things we usually check out with any behaviour is, "What's normal for this age?" Bedwetting in five-year-olds is pretty common. We think about 70 per cent of four-year-olds wet the bed often, and 40 per cent of kids of school age still do sometimes.

Other parents piped up from the group, "Yes, one of ours still does too."

"So it's fairly normal, but that doesn't mean you should just ignore it," we added.

Next you check other possible causes:
1. Medical. Is there any physical problem – bladder capacity, muscle problems, urinary tract infection, diabetes. It's a good idea to eliminate all of these possibilities with your doctor.
"We've done all that!" said Harry.
2. Psychological. Is there any big stress in his life? Or something he might not have told you about?
3. Has he shown that he can control it? Does he sometimes have dry beds? Where and when?
4. Is there a pay off? For instance, does he get to see you in the middle of the night while he doesn't see you much in the day? Who washes the sheets?

Helping your child

We talked around this with Margaret and Harry. Harry was surprised there could be other reasons than just "laziness". Margaret, however, was starting to feel like getting tough! Now it was time for the third step – deciding to act. The whole group weighed in with things

The sensuous child

Experienced parents have noticed that, around the age of three or four, children often show heightened sensual awareness.

Parents can feel confused and worried when their son or daughter exhibits behaviour which can even look seductive. Parents have often told us they observed:

★ ***little girls putting beads*** or other objects into their vagina and enjoying the feeling as they walk around
★ ***children wanting privacy*** in the toilet, while they experiment with their faeces
★ ***children rubbing their genitals*** against a parent's body during play
★ ***the classic case of children*** playing "doctors" inside a cupboard with another child.

Sandra, 32 "One morning, when we were having a cuddle in bed, my four-year-old son got on top of me and was very smoochy, and said in a seductive kind of voice, 'We're making love, aren't we, Mummy?' (He has a book about how babies are made, so I knew where the concept had come from.) I was really shocked, but put him down off the bed and said, 'No, we're not; only grown-ups make love.' I tried to make it firm, but not too harsh. He went off to play and seemed happy enough. My husband and I made a practice of getting up in the morning and sitting with our son on the couch, reading or talking for our close time instead of being in the bed. After a while, we went back to normal behaviour and the problem passed."

This seems to be a brief phase, if it is handled matter of factly, by redirecting them to other forms of play. A sensible approach here can avoid habits building up.

that had worked for them, or other people they had heard of, and Margaret and Harry added their ideas too. They came up with the following possibilities:

★ visit the toilet just before going to bed
★ see a doctor again just to double check. Choose a doctor with commonsense who won't make a big deal of it. Or ask for a referral to a special clinic for this problem. This is where you will find the most up-to-date information.
★ use a wetness alarm, available from pharmacies
★ have a good think about whether Jason may have "secret" worries, from school or elsewhere. This is especially important if the bedwetting problem is new. Ask about this in a caring and undramatic way. Listen to him, and talk to his teacher about how he is

generally at school. You don't need to explain why you need to know
* leave the light on in the hall and toilet, or a potty near the bed with a tiny night light beside it
* consider homeopathic or osteopathic treatment
* for a few nights, let him sleep on a mattress on the floor beside your bed, so he can wake you for help if he wants to do a wee. If you hear him stirring in the night, you can wake him and sit him on the toilet. Help and praise him if he wakes you up and gets it right
* give rewards for dry nights, put stars on a chart towards a zoo trip or other treat
* let him know where clean bedding and pyjamas are kept. Make it his job to help himself in the night by putting wet bedding in a separate bin to be washed, and changing into something dry. (Older kids above six can start the washing machine before school.)

There were certainly a lot of options to choose from. Harry decided to spend time with Jason at bedtime, and also to have a good talk to him about school. Margaret was pleased about that, and she decided to try some new ideas – stop changing the sheets for Jason, and to have a star chart for his successes (a reward for five dry nights). The secret to any problem like this is to be creative and keep experimenting. When we have the chance to talk with other experienced parents, we can usually find new options – things we haven't yet tried, but may well help us and our child's situation.

The end of the day

It was getting dark outside when the parenting course ended for the day. We were amazed when we thought about how much goes into making those little four-year-olds what they are, and how much learning and growing they do at this tender age. As leaders of the course we felt comfortable that, while we had offered some clarity, it was the collective wisdom and sheer warmth and friendliness of these parents for each other that would help them most with their families, as they headed off into the night to be with them again.

Good things to try

Confidence with doctors and dentists

Your child can become familiar and comfortable with these visits by seeing you being examined by a doctor and having your teeth checked by a dentist. Having another adult along helps with this.

Preferably, don't take your child when you are having wisdom teeth removed – a straightforward check-up would be best! Before you go, explain simply what is going to happen. If you like, you can ring the receptionist beforehand or ask when you arrive if your child can watch and learn. Surprisingly, we can often teach ourselves to be more calm, positive and relaxed when we are busy putting on a show to reassure our child.

Many dentists and doctors are friendly and interested in children, and know the benefits of having a child who feels at ease. Dentists even let children sit in the chair and show them the "magic" toothbrushes which tickle their fingers. Your child is getting to know a familiar face and name of the doctor or dentist; they will have seen and tried some of the equipment and, importantly, have heard the noises and smelt the smells in an atmosphere of adventure and interest. If more of us had this positive experience as children, we would be happier patients.

Soon, your child will be saying: "I want to see Dr Stone, he'll make my ache better" or "I like Val, she's my best dentist."

Sue, 26 "I was on my way to the doctor for a breast examination and was trying to think how to explain this to my three-year-old because he wants to know about everything. So I said, 'The doctor wants to check parts of my body to see if they are all working well' and I told him he'd probably look at my eyes, ears, chest, heart and breasts. In the waiting room, my son said, in a very loud voice, 'Mummy, is doctor going to feel your breasts?' I said: 'Yes, now where are the blocks?' trying to distract him and hoping the other patients hadn't really heard. But it got worse. 'Does doctor like to feel your breasts, mummy?' Well, they heard that time!"

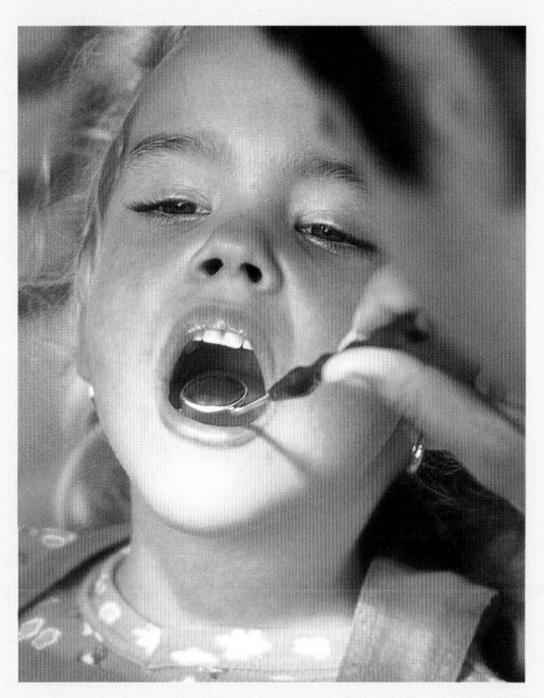

Preparing for school

Before you know it your child is approaching five, and it's time to start thinking about school. Everything you have done with your child up to this age has helped them to get "school ready". They will already have mastered, or be well on the way to mastering, such "school-useful" skills as:

- ★ recognizing and perhaps writing their name
- ★ concentrating for reasonable amounts of time (this helps with listening to stories and carrying out activities in the classroom)
- ★ knowing how to go to the toilet and wash their hands
- ★ knowing to wait when an adult is busy talking to someone else and then take their turn to speak (this takes lots of practice and reminders!)
- ★ recognizing what they are feeling, and knowing how to use words to ask for what they want
- ★ knowing their parents' names, and home address
- ★ knowing to stay away from strangers, the road and busy traffic
- ★ putting on a hat before going outside to play to protect from the sun or cold
- ★ knowing the importance of not hurting other people, or themselves
- ★ some "fine motor skills" – such as cutting, pasting, drawing, threading, building with blocks – and some "gross motor skills", including running, jumping, hopping and climbing.

Most children will be good at some of these and not others. You can give practical help and encouragement with the ones that they might need to practise, and which you think they might need.

Good things to try

Helping to build motor skills

These ideas were collated by the specialist teacher at our local school, Mrs Robbie Poynter. Use them in a fun way, without pressure, and your child is sure to enjoy them and come back for more.

- ★ ***Tidy Mum's sewing basket.*** Rewind the cottons and roll up the wool. Make pom-poms (big, small, rainbow, for hats, clown noses and buttons). Sew buttons onto strips of material. Draw pictures onto cardboard, punch holes and sew around.
- ★ ***Put pegs around an*** (empty) icecream container or an old tin with a thin, smooth edge. How many can you peg on your clothes? Help Mum peg out the washing, doll's or teddy bear's clothes.
- ★ ***Tie a balloon to a fairly short*** piece of string. Hold onto the end of the string and bat the inflated balloon back and forth with your hand. Extend the length of string, hit back and forth to a partner, without letting it touch the floor.
- ★ ***Suspend a tennis ball*** on elastic from a tree limb, verandah or monkey bar, and practise hitting it with a cheap, light bat.
- ★ ***Play with a yo-yo,*** winding up the string, dropping and returning the yo-yo to your hand.
- ★ ***Play hand soccer*** by rolling a tennis ball around the floor, aiming between two objects, like tins or mugs, for goals. Toss ball from hand to hand. Pass the ball from hand to hand around tummy, legs and then in reverse direction.
- ★ ***Play tiddly winks.*** Aim into a saucer, bowl or cup.
- ★ ***Roll marbles.*** Push, drop down pipes and tubes.
- ★ ***Bounce a tennis ball*** and catch it in a small container.
- ★ ***Hammer nails.***
- ★ ***Thread buttons.***
- ★ ***Knit.***
- ★ ***Build with blocks,*** manipulative toys, nuts and bolts.
- ★ ***Decorate cakes with sultanas,*** small pieces of chocolate and silver cachous.
- ★ ***Fold paper – origami*** and paper planes.
- ★ ***Dismantle old appliances*** to see how they work (watch your telephone and television set!). Get some old phones from the phone company, record players, and so on. Pull them to bits— unscrew, unwind, twist off. It's amazing how many parts make up a telephone.
- ★ ***Plant seeds and flowers*** and watch for them to come up.
- ★ ***Peel oranges and pod peas.***

Good things to try

Fun with numbers

There are dozens of ways you can bring numbers into your day-to-day activities together. Start with the smallest numbers and relate them to things your child knows; for example, when putting on their socks, count them – one-two, two shoes; putting on their jumper – one arm, two arms. When you give them pieces of fruit, count them out as you put them on the plate – one, two, three.

★ ***Ask questions relating*** to their body, so they can look and feel to find the answer. How many fingers are on your hand? How many ears do you have? Do this in a playful way – on car trips or in the bath.

★ ***While you are driving in the car,*** a five-year-old will often enjoy answering funny questions. How many legs do two dogs have? Three cows? If I put four chocolates and two artichokes on a plate for morning tea, how many would be left for me and how many would you take?

★ ***At the supermarket,*** give your child a shopping bag and ask them to collect four oranges for you or six apples.

★ ***Find natural "counters"*** to add and subtract with: fill a large wooden bowl with shiny smooth chestnuts, or delightfully scented pinecones or smooth round pebbles. Then these will be useful for making patterns, putting into clusters of the same number, and for adding and subtracting.

★ ***Make a child's telephone list*** with photos next to each person's phone number, for example, Nanna or their friend up the road. You could use drawings instead of photos. Teach your child to memorize the emergency phone number. Stress to them never to use it, except in an emergency.

It helps if you believe that maths is really easy when you know how. There are no "hard" sums – they are all easy when you know how, so don't even use the word hard when you do sums with them.

Hopefully, by the time they start school they will have had opportunities to play with other children of their own age, and have some experience with sharing, being friendly and enjoying time together.

They will also, hopefully, be able to do what the teacher instructs them to do. But don't expect the teacher to have a magic wand. If you haven't taught your child to carry out instructions, the teacher may not be able to either. Children of school age should ideally have already spent some time in other people's homes or in the care of trusted adults other than their parents. This way they will have had the chance to get used to being in a new place without you and know that you can be relied on to return.

Familiarization with the school

You and your child need to feel comfortable with the school, so check it out as follows:

★ observe whether the kids look happy and play well, or whether there are angry-looking cliques and a lack of spontaneous happy play
★ check whether the staff are reasonably relaxed, or whether they are overworked and underappreciated
★ make sure the school has a reasonable standard of cleanliness, and safety measures such as boundary fences
★ find out what other parents think of the school
★ ask to meet your child's teacher
★ visit the school a couple of times, and walk around so that you both get used to the physical setting – the size, smell and sounds
★ take your child to the toilets
★ take your child on a boundary walk so they have physically gone around the inside boundary fences and can look back to see the position of the class rooms from different directions
★ let your child play on the play equipment – it's a big drawcard!
★ help your child rehearse saying the teacher's name

★ it certainly helps to have a friend to start school with – if you are new to the area, ask the principal to suggest a local family you could make contact with and then the kids could become friends before school begins
★ remember that if you are confident and enthusiastic about your child going to school, it is highly likely they will feel good about it too.

Reading preparation

The best way to help a child learn to read is to have them first fall in love with stories. Babies and children love having stories read to them. Find books which you enjoy, with pictures that are pleasant for you to look at (five hundred times!). Keep looking for new books; use libraries or shop at jumble sales and markets, where you can go home with a shopping bag full of books for a small amount of money.

★ **Let them see you reading.** They'll notice how you

For the first few days of school be organised so you don't have to rush, and make sure you are on time to pick them up.

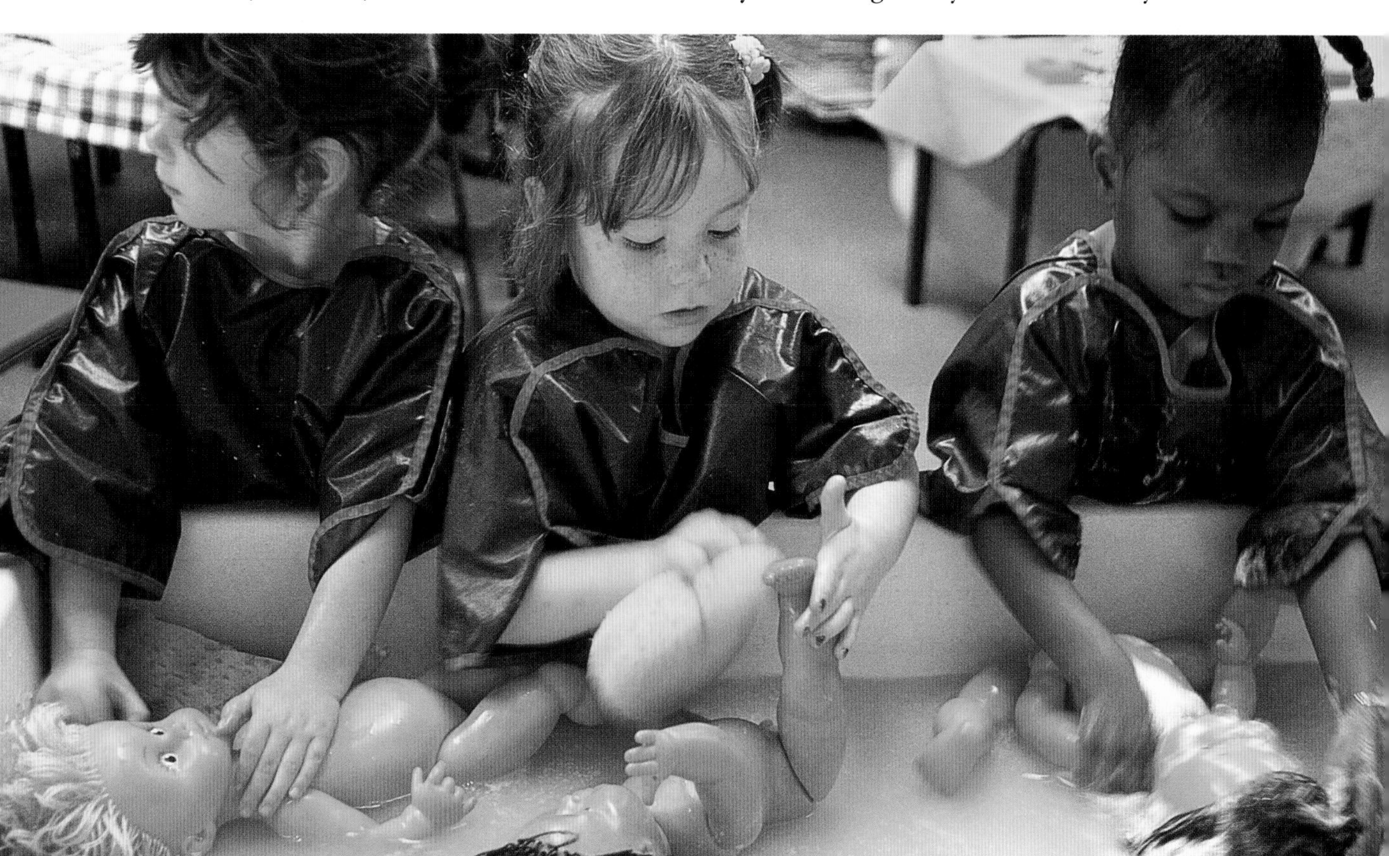

Good things to try

Memory improvement

As children get closer to school age, they need to be able to remember what they have been asked to do and to get things in order. For instance: "Finish your drink, put the cup on the sink, then do your hair." By using this game as practice from a very young age, they can build up their confidence and ability to remember a series of instructions and carry them out independently. Over time, make it harder. The following are approximate ages and suggestions of what can be taught:

★ **1½–2½** "Go into my bedroom and get my red slippers, please."

★ **2½–3½** "Go to Daddy in the kitchen and ask what time it is, then come and tell me."

★ **3½–4½** "Go and see where the big and little hands of the clock are pointing, then come and tell me and I'll tell you what time it is."

You'll notice that children love to help and can get things for you, and will be proud of remembering. If you are pinned down feeding a baby, your toddler can bring you a biscuit or get a nappy from the basket, and you will appreciate the help.

concentrate and become engrossed in your magazine, newspaper or book; how you sometimes laugh or talk about a part of the book with others. You can tell them what your book is about and that they can read it one day, too.

★ **Play the "my word" game.** Once a day, ask your child to choose something in the house. Make a sign with that word clearly printed on it and let them stick it on the object. After a week, collect the signs and see if your child can return them to the right places. To help a younger child, you can draw the object on the back of the sign as a clue.

★ **Play "word snap".** Together, choose the names of people your child likes, then make pairs of cards with these names printed on them. Shuffle the cards and deal equal numbers to you and your child. First, the child puts one down, then you put one of yours next to it. Does it match? Yes, "snap". The first one to see the match and say "snap" wins. You can also spread out the cards face up and together find the ones which are the same.

- ★ **Invent rhyme and rhythm games.** Reading is about enjoying words. As you walk together, get the rhythm going. "We are... walking... up the... hill. Peter... is the... fastest... one. I am... catching... up with him." Make funny rhyming words; for example, using Peter's name. "Peter, neater, sweeter, meet her."
- ★ **Leave notes.** In the morning, the child finds a large, simple note on the bedroom floor. It includes signs or drawings to give a clue to the message. "Hello!" (picture, person waving) "I love you!" (heart). "Boo!" (surround with dots). The signs become more challenging as the child gets older: "Good morning. Come to our bed at..." (picture of clock with hands pointing to 8 o'clock).

Cause for celebration

The first day of school is one to celebrate. Plan something special as a gift to yourselves as parents. This signifies an important milestone. You have spent thousands of hours caring, guiding and helping, thinking about and working

for this five-year-old who is now launched into their school years. Congratulations!!!

Signifying changes

Growing up is an achievement that you can make special in your child's eyes. Each birthday signals that a whole year of learning has gone by and that the child is an older and different person from the previous year. Some parents like to spend time with their child, on or after a birthday, going through the child's room and putting away or giving away those things they have outgrown – clothes, toys, books and pictures. (But be careful not to do this with precious or important possessions.)

This clearing out and remaking of their environment helps children to notice changes in themselves and to celebrate their achievements. The freshness and newness of their surroundings helps them to feel fresh and new too.

Ways in which parents "signify" their child's growing up can include:

★ at an appropriate time, put away or store away "baby things" (a special blanket, for instance)
★ expect and reward dry beds by giving your child a bed of their own
★ change baby words you have used and remind them to use the proper words. For example, no longer ask, "Do you want a bowl of yummies?" but "Do you want some breakfast cereal?"
★ once they have learned how to solve problems with friends, don't rush in to rescue them in their play with another child. Remind them that they know what to do and send them back to fix it
★ buy a school bag, even though they are only in nursery
★ start giving them pocket money and helping them to use it.

Proud to be growing up

If you have a baby and an older child, it's a good idea to give special privileges to the older one – staying up a little later or doing grown-up things, like going to the shops with you while the baby is minded. This will send a signal that you value maturity and that being older pays. This way, you won't have two or more children competing to be babylike and it will be fair in the long run, as younger children grow and earn privileges. But, in the short term, special benefits associated with being older will compensate for the time-consuming nature of the younger children and make the older one feel special and want to be more helpful.

> "*We had saved up for this day. We kept all our one-pound coins from our change in a jar and, on the first day our daughter was at school, Max and I went out for a champagne lunch at a restaurant overlooking the city. I'd never done anything so extravagant and it felt like total luxury. We talked over the good times and what had seemed like big problems which had now faded away. We realized a lot of parenting lay ahead, but we had reached a big milestone. We had done it together. The day was a great memory to keep for both of us.*"
>
> ***Clare, 35***

harmony and happiness

How can parents nurture their child's spiritual development? Here are some ways in which we help our children (and ourselves) to appreciate the fullness of life.

Compassion

This means considering the feelings of other people and living things. By thinking this way, we are able to act with kindness arising from empathy. Little children have lots of natural compassion – they hate to see an animal hurting or a younger child crying, for instance. You can help strengthen compassion by teaching them how to notice the feelings of others and to show gentleness towards insects, animals, and so on. When they show small acts of kindness, comment on them. And, of course, treat your children kindly, so that they experience the feeling of receiving care.

Harmony with nature

Enjoy the outdoors together. Watch the sunrise or, at night, go into the woods to hear and see the animals. Sit quietly with them in wild places. Go camping. Grow plants. Recycle. Celebrate each changing season with decorations, cooking, collecting leaves, flowers and stones.

Optimism

Talk about the beauty and happiness around us. Strictly limit television watching and computer games. Children under five should not have to see the images and hear the messages on the news, for instance. They are able to understand, but cannot appreciate the context of these things and will get a frightening and distorted view of the world. This can lead to behaviour problems, such as aggression, as they try to cope with their inner fears. This isn't a matter of painting a false picture; the world is largely positive, with a majority of safe, trustworthy people. There are real problems in the world, but worrying about them is adults' work, not little children's. When you discuss problems, talk about what you, as a family, can do about them. Teach them concepts which you want them to take on; for example, "there is some good in everyone", "things have a way of working out" and "for every problem there is a solution" can be mentioned quietly and will become part of their attitude.

Appreciating differences

Where possible, expose your children naturally and easily to people of different ages, disabilities, races and talents. Talk about your own "disabilities", so they realise that these are normal and surmountable. As they are growing up, show them that you value people of different races, cultures, beliefs, sexual preferences, and so on.

Forgiveness and problem-solving

Self-esteem and confidence come not from being perfect, but from being able to take a mistake or setback and think your way around it. Children can learn to take responsibility for their actions without having to cover up mistakes or not try for fear of failure. You can say, "Well, that was a mistake, but I'm sure you can fix it up." When a problem arises, help them with brainstorming possible options and try different solutions until you find one that works. This will give your children a "can do" approach to life which will become part of their character forever.

Wellness

Expect and help children to take care of their bodies, because they are important and valuable. Talk about how their bodies are strong and well, and how they have lots of energy. Point out how good children are at healing quickly. Place high value on their diet, exercise and safety, such as always fastening their seatbelts in the car. This all says, "You are precious."

Peacefulness

Encourage concentration by allowing children to play uninterrupted and absorb themselves in learning. Have a quiet house, at least some of the time. Teach your children relaxation using stories, tapes and by relaxing touch.

Open-mindedness

All people matter. You can demonstrate this by always greeting your children by name and saying goodbye individually. They, in turn, say "Hello", always adding the person's name if they know it, and "Good morning" and "Good night" to each person in the home. All points of view matter. Don't put down people, groups, religions or races in front of your children. Point out that ideas and beliefs change. They might believe one way now and another later. In answer to questions, tell them, "Some people believe ... while others think ..." When they ask you for an answer, don't always give them your views. Ask them what they think, and why.

Self-acceptance

This quality arises out of being accepted unconditionally in your own family. If you have experienced acceptance as a child, you will go into the world expecting it and usually getting it, because you radiate this assurance. Give loving messages clearly and unambiguously: "I'm glad you are here in this family; it's great to have you around." Of course, you will criticize and seek to change behaviour, but always separate this from the person. "I don't like what you are doing." You can even put compliments into your criticisms. "You are far smarter than that. I know you can think of a better way to solve the argument. Let's see you do it."

Happiness

Help children to value others' happiness as well as their own. "Look how happy Suzie is with the present you gave her." "I like being with you, you are really good fun." We all aim to give our children a happy childhood, but the eventual message we want them to have is that happiness is a choice. Point out the ways they know to help themselves feel happy – playing with their favourite toys; inviting other children to play with them; sitting and being peaceful for a while with a book or toy; having a bath and playing in it. We can actively encourage even young children by routinely using statements like, "Have a happy time", "enjoy yourself", "find something you'd like to do."

Spiritual practices

We adults may have spiritual practices of our own, having discovered how much they help our lives. Some people go to church, others meditate or do yoga; some observe family rituals, follow special diets, gather for study or discussion and so on. We believe that children can be encouraged to try, stick with and, as they grow older, find out for themselves the potential benefits of spiritual practices. With some flexibility to accommodate young children's needs, spiritual practices in childhood can remain a positive memory. These activities also create a "spiritual space" in a child's mind which, as a teenager and adult, they can build on in their own way. They will know that there is more meaning to life than possessions, approval or outer success, and will be hardier and more self-directed.

The above is an abbreviated guide to a huge subject. Perhaps the biggest challenge for us, when we acknowledge that our children have a need for spiritual guidance from us, is to work out how this is expressed in our lives. Whatever we say to them won't matter as much as what they notice about our serenity, our compassion, our free-spiritedness and our happiness in the world. Which is quite a challenge!

Bless the road

Now in a while my precious child
You will unfurl your wings
Be sure to learn each twist and turn
And weave your mystical rings
And before you go, be sure to know
You're part of everything
Your heart is strong, your journey long
Now listen to this song I sing

Then go in peace and grow in grace and goodness
Know that you have nothing to fear
And dry your eyes my little one
And let there be no tears
Send me a dreaming from where you go
I promise I shall hear
Oh beautiful, beloved soul companion
Thank you for those beautiful years

And heaven hold and watch your way forever
May your every dream come true
Forgive all wrong, always be strong
And do what you must do
You stand before this open door
And you must now go through
My precious friend
My own, my sweet companion
Bless the road that carries you.

By Steve Cooney
Kindly adapted by Steve Cooney from his song *Bless the Road*.
Performed by Mary Black on her album *Speaking With the Angel*

Useful addresses

Association for Postnatal Illness
Helpline: 020 7386 0868
Advises and offers emotional support to sufferers of post-natal depression and their families.

BLISS
Tel: 020 7820 9471
A support network for parents of babies who require intensive or special care, providing emotional and practical support.

British Association for Counselling
Tel: 01788 550899
Produces a nationwide list of qualified counsellors.

Caesarean Support Network
Tel: 01624 661 269
(Monday–Friday, after 6 pm and weekends)
Provides emotional support and practical advice for mothers who have had or who may need a Caesarean.

Child Support Agency
Tel: 0345 133 133 (enquiry line)
In Northern Ireland: 01232 896896
A Government-funded agency that assesses maintenance levels for parents who no longer live with their children.

Children 1st
Tel: 0131 337 8539
A Scottish organization providing practical advice and support to parents on the everyday care of babies and children.

Contact-a-Family
Helpline: 020 7383 3555
(9 am–5.30 pm)
Offers parents with children who have special needs or disabilities a chance to contact other families in similar circumstances for mutual advice and support.

Council for Disabled Children
Tel: 020 7843 6061/6058
An information line for parents on all aspects of disability.

EPOCH
Tel: 020 7700 0627
Provides written material on discipline and alternatives to smacking.

Foundation for the Study of Infant Deaths
(Cot death research and support)
Tel: 020 7235 0965
Helpline: 020 7235 1721
Provides support for parents and families who has suffered the sudden bereavement of a baby. Also provides the most up-to-date guidelines and research on how to help prevent cot death.

Gingerbread
Tel: 020 7336 8183
In Northern Ireland: 01232 231417
A support line for single parents that provides practical everyday help.

Health Education Authority
Tel: 020 7222 5300
Publications: 01235 465 565
In Scotland: Tel: 0131 536 5500
Publishes books and leaflets on a whole range of areas relating to the family.

Home-Start UK
Tel: 0116 233 9955
In Northern Ireland: 01232 460772
Voluntary organization that offers guidance and practical and emotional support for families starting up their own homes.

International Association of Infant Massage – UK
Tel: 020 8591 1399
Website: www.iaim.org.uk
Provides a nationwide list of qualified infant massage teachers.

La Leche League of Great Britain
Tel: 020 7242 1278
Support and information for women experiencing problems with breastfeeding.

Meet-a-Mum Association (MAMA)
Tel: 020 8771 5595
Helpline: 020 8768 0123
(Monday–Friday 7pm–10pm)
An organization for women suffering from postnatal depression, offering practical advice and counselling.

National Childbirth Trust (NCT)
Enquiry line: 020 8992 8637
Website: www.nct-online.org
Provides nationwide antenatal classes and also runs postnatal support groups.

National Childminding Association
Advice line: 020 8466 0200

National Council for One Parent Families
Tel: 020 7267 1361
Lone Parent line:
0800 018 5026
Maintenance and Money Line:
020 7428 5424

NEWPIN (New Parent and Infant Network)
Tel: 020 7703 6326
Support line for parents suffering from stress.

NICMA (Northern Ireland)
Tel: 01247 811015
Information line with details on child care services and facilities.

NIPPA (Northern Ireland)
Tel: 01232 662825
Provides information on professional child care and education services.

NSPCC
NSPCC National Centre
42 Curtain Road
London EC2A 3NH
Tel: 020 7825 2500
Helpline: 0800 800 500
Website: www.nspcc.org.uk
Leading national charity concerned with the protection of and prevention of cruelty to children.

Osteopathic Centre for Children
Tel: 020 7486 6160
Information on osteopathic practices.
For a list of local osteopaths phone: 020 7799 2599

Parentline
Helpline: 0808 800 2222
A parent network providing support and courses for anyone in a parenting role.

Parents Advice Centre (Northern Ireland)
Tel: 01232 238800

Parents in Partnership – Parent Infant Network (PIPPIN)
Tel: 01992 471 355
Offers families advice and support on parent-baby relationships in the period before and after the birth.

Serene (including the Cry-sis helpline)
Helpline: 020 7404 5011
(8 am–11 pm)
Provides support and practical advice to parents who are finding it hard to cope with their baby's excessive crying, broken sleep and constant demands.

Stillbirth and Neonatal Death Society (SANDS)
Tel: 020 7436 5881
Provides nationwide support groups for bereaved parents.

Twins and Multiple Births Association (TAMBA)
Helpline: 0173 286 8000
An organization for parents of twins or more that aims to put families in touch with other, providing mutual support and advice.

Women's Aid
Helpline: 0345 023 468
(Northern Ireland):
01232 331 818

Index

E

F

G

H

I

P

Q

R

S

T

U V

W

Y

Acknowledgments

Authors' acknowledgments
This book was a huge effort by a committed team of people. At Dorling Kindersley, Daphne Razazan, Lynne Brown and Corinne Roberts performed superhuman efforts to try and meet our needs for a book that was human, clear, readable, and that departed from the magazine-perfect image portrayed in many parenting books today.

Caroline Greene, Dawn Bates, Rajen Shah, Mercedes Morgan, Claire Cross and Richard Czapnik were friendly under pressure, creative, and optimistic in getting text, pictures, and cartoons to flow together well.

For their stories, words, quotes and ideas for our earlier manuscript *The Mother and Baby Book*, we are grateful to many hundreds of parents and friends over the twenty years we have been working in parent workshops, clinics, and the media. You made this book credible, rich and worthwhile.

For the great parenting tradition that has refused to let society's madness be imposed on children without protest – Ben Spock, Penelope Leach, Thakur Balach Bramachiri, organizations like Parent Network, and all the networks of loving parents and professionals around the world who work to protect and preserve children and families.

Permissions and additional material
For permission to use extracts from his book *Family Matters* (originally published by Collins Dove in Australia, and hopefully soon to be reprinted) we are very grateful to Martin Flanagan, sports and feature writer with the *Melbourne Age*, and a wonderful craftsman of words and of the heart.

Parent humour sweeps the world and is valued by all, but the originators are often lost. We appreciate the great jokes gained from internet chat lists, and apologize for not being able to accredit their authors.

For his words from *Letter to Daniel* published by Penguin Books, UK, used in the frontispiece, we are grateful to Fergal Keane.

For his beautiful recordings of his own baby son, and the detailed information on ages and language abilities of young children, we are indebted to Peter Downes, former comprehensive school head and currently a modern languages and boys education consultant based in Huntingdon, Cambridgeshire.

For her ideas on sorting out mixed feelings in pregnancy, we are indebted to Elizabeth Mellor.

For their story of a first birth experience we thank Dianne and Ian Mallett, and Amy, Joel, Julian and Beth.

For the information on combinations of high-need babies and high-need mothers we are grateful to William Sears and his books including *Keys to Calming The Fussy Baby* published by Barron's and available from Amazon.com.

For his generous permission to use the words of the song *Bless the Road*, and amend it for our needs, we are truly grateful to Australian Irish musician Steve Cooney. *Bless the Road* is sung by Mary Black on her album *Speaking with the Angel* (Grapevine Label Limited). Copyright Dara Records Ltd., Dublin.

Dorling Kindersley would like to thank:
editorial assistance – Corinne Asghar, Claire Cross and Caroline Greene
design assistance – Ted Kinsey and Bernhard Koppmeyer
proofreading – Valerie Kitchenham
index – Hilary Bird
photography – Mike Good, Jenny Matthews, Sally Smallwood and Adrian Weinbrecht
picture research – Anna Grapes
illustrations – Richard Collins

Photography credits:
Bubbles: Moose Azim 61b, 65; Ian West 150tr
Collections: Sandra Lousada 10-11, 72bl, 72br, 73bl, 73br, 121, 137br; Kim Naylor 15t, 130cl; Anthea Sieveking 57tr
Family Life Picture Library/Angela Hampton: 113tr, 113cr, 113br, 230tl
Image Bank: Tosca Radigonda 135cr
Eddie Lawrence: 35tr, 52t, 53r, 63tr, 143, 147b, 162bl
Mother & Baby Picture Library: Paul Mitchell 14
Network Photographers Ltd: Jennie Matthews 118-119, 168, 231br
Photofusion: David Tothill 218cr
Powerstock/Zefa: Bill Whelan 14t
SOA Photo Agency: Peisl/Picture Press 29t; Raith/Picture Press 109; Steiner/Picture Press 129t
The Stock Market: Randy M. Ury 42-43
Tony Stone Images: Bruce Ayres 98tl; Dan Bosler 184tl; Jo Browne/Mick Smee 166-167; Peter Cade 50t, 88tr; Frank Clarkson 22, 27; Bruce Fier 116-117; Alain Garsmeur 14-15; Penny Gentieu 15b, 48b; Roy Gumpel 212t; Klaus Lahnstein 217br; Eric Larrayadieu 144t; Sarah Lawless 157br; Rosanne Olson 208tr; Niyati Reeve 134tr; Tamara Reynolds 80tl, 195; Andy Sacks 221br; Timothy Shonnard 132c; Mark Williams 44b
Telegraph Colour Library: Guillaume Bouzonnet 233; R. Chapple 16br; FPG International 16cl; Daniel Kron 17cl; Antonio Mo 17cb; Simon Potter 17br; Rag Productions Inc 18l; Ken Ross 15t; Arthur Tilley 17bl; V.C.L 180tl; Mel Yates 123bl

Picture Research: Anna Grapes

RECOMMENDED READING

Understanding your child....
Whats Going On in There? How the Brain and Mind Develop in the First Five Years of Life – Lise Eliot, Penguin Press, 2000
Your Baby and Child – Penelope Leach, Penguin, 1997
Education for Special Needs – Principles and Practice in Camp Hill Schools, Henning Hansmann, Floris Books, UK, 1992
Baby Massage – Nicky Bainbridge & Dr. Alan Heath, Dorling Kindersley, UK, 2000
Father Time – Making Time for Your Children – Daniel Petre, Pan Macmillan Sydney, 1998
Crying – Anna McGrail, National Childbirth Trust, 1999
Your Kids are Worth it – Barbara Coloroso, Lothian, 1995
Nature's Masterpiece – A Family Survival Book – Libby Purves, Hodder, 2000

The big picture...
Children First – Penelope Leach, Penguin, 1994

Creative activities with children...
Toymaking with Children – Freya Jaffke, Floris Books, 1988
Feltcraft – Making Dolls, Gifts and Toys – Petra Berger, Floris Books, 1994
Earthwise – Environmental Crafts and Activities with Young Children – Carol Petrash, Floris Books, 1992
The Children's Year – Cooper, Fynes-Clinton and Rowling, Hawthorn Press, 1986

Steve and Shaaron's books include...
Raising Boys – why boys are different and how to help them become happy and well-balanced men – Thorsons UK, 1998
Manhood – a book about setting men free – Hawthorn Press UK 1997
The Secret of Happy Children – Thorsons UK, 1998
More Secrets of Happy Children – Thorsons UK, 1999
How Love Works – Thorsons UK, 1999